Two-Hour Mini Quilt Projects

Two-Hour Mini Quilt Projects

Over 111 Appliquéd & Pieced Designs

McKenzie Kate

Sterling Publishing Co., Inc. New York
A Sterling/Chapelle Book

For Chapelle

Owner: *Jo Packham*

Editor: *Malissa M. Boatwright*

Special thanks to Cathy Sexton for her valuable consultation.

Staff: *Kass Burchett, Rebecca Christensen, Marilyn Goff, Amber Hansen, Shirley Heslop, Holly Hollingsworth, Susan Jorgensen, Susan Laws, Barbara Milburn, Karmen Quinney, Leslie Ridenour, Cindy Rooks, and Cindy Stoeckl*

Photographer: *Kevin Dilley for Hazen Photography*

Photography Styling: *Susan Laws, Jo Packham, and Cindy Rooks*

If you have any questions or comments or would like information on specialty products featured in this book, please contact: Chapelle, Ltd. • P.O. Box 9252 • Ogden, UT 84409 • (801) 621-2777 • Fax (801) 621-2788

Library of Congress Cataloging-in-Publication Data

Kate, McKenzie.
   Two-hour mini quilt projects : over 111 appliquéd & pieced designs
 / McKenzie Kate.
      p.   cm.
   "A Sterling/Chapelle book."
   Includes index.
   ISBN 0-8069-8643-3
   1. Patchwork--Patterns. 2. Quilting--Patterns. 3. Appliqué-
 -Patterns. 4. Miniature quilts. I. Title.
 TT835.K38 1997
 746.46'041--dc20
                                                96-34596
                                                CIP

A Sterling/Chapelle Book

10 9 8 7 6 5 4

First paperback edition published in 1998 by
Sterling Publishing Company, Inc.
387 Park Avenue South, New York, N.Y. 10016
© 1997 by Chapelle Limited
Distributed in Canada by Sterling Publishing
℅ Canadian Manda Group, One Atlantic Avenue, Suite 105
Toronto, Ontario, Canada M6K 3E7
Distributed in Great Britain and Europe by Cassell PLC
Wellington House, 125 Strand, London WC2R 0BB, England
Distributed in Australia by Capricorn Link (Australia) Pty Ltd.
P.O. Box 6651, Baulkham Hills, Business Centre, NSW 2153, Australia
Printed in China
All rights reserved

Sterling ISBN 0-8069-8643-3 Trade
                0-8069-8705-7 Paper

Contents

About the Designers

Debra Crabtree-Lewis

Kathy Distefano-Griffiths

Debra was born in Spanish Fork, Utah. She is the mother of six and stepmother of five. She currently lives in Springville, Utah, with her husband, Keith, six of their children, and a dog.

Debra's mother and grandmother taught her to love nature when she was very young. She grew up on a farm and learned the name of every herb, flower, and vegetable that grew there.

She has always enjoyed making dolls from sticks and all types of make-believe things from hollyhock petals. A collector at heart, she sees beauty in everything.

Debra's art has been published in craft books and kits for about 10 years and her designs are featured on pages 16 to 43.

Kathy is the mother of four children, ranging in ages from 20 to 28, and the grandmother of two.

She graduated from Brigham Young University in Provo, Utah, majoring in art education and taught art in the public school system for several years. She also taught decorative painting for eight years, focusing on European folk arts.

Kathy has designed and marketed a hand-painted gift line for the past seven years and her art has been published in soft-bound craft books since 1987. Her designs are featured on pages 44 to 71.

About the Designers

Emily Dinsdale

Rebecca Carter

Emily was born and raised in central Utah. She currently resides in Springville, Utah, with her husband, Jeff, and youngest daughter, Allison. She also has two other daughters, Melissa and Andrea, and has a beautiful grand-daughter, McKenna, who is the light of her life.

She is a devoted wife, mother, and a wonderful friend to all who know her.

Emily is always transforming some tin pot or shelf into a work of beauty. One of her favorite hobbies is collecting miniatures. She loves to put miniature bunnies to bed in a walnut shell or tucked into an old lace hanky.

Her designs are featured on pages 72 to 99.

Rebecca was born and raised in Bountiful, Utah, the only girl of nine children. Rebecca and her husband, Rick, live in Salem, Utah, with their three children, Rachel, Tyrel, and Chantry. They enjoy the quiet life of Salem and peaceful bike rides along the canals which overlook the valley.

Rebecca is a graduate of Southern Utah State University. She majored in fine arts and has a three-year degree in interior design.

Rebecca has taught calligraphy and art classes, but now spends her time designing fabrics, craft books for the decorative painter, and pattern books for appliqué, woodcraft, and clip-art. Her art is available on electronic clip-art and on rubber stamps and her newest designs are featured on pages 100 to 126.

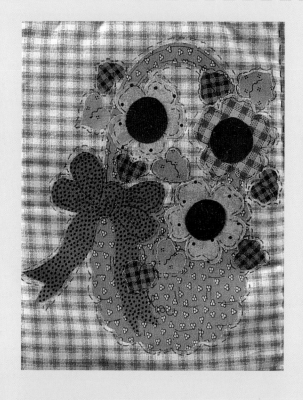

General Instructions

This section explains the techniques and general definitions to be used to create the projects in this book. The basic construction, additional techniques, and embroidery stitches used are thoroughly detailed and diagrammed on pages 10-14, and are referenced at the beginning of each project for ease in determining which techniques will be used on individual projects throughout this book. General definitions are provided on page 15.

Each photographed project has been created so it can be reproduced exactly from the designer's model. However, each project can be finished in many ways to create a more personalized piece. There are several additional project ideas at the end of each designer's section; they also have been designed to be used as actual pattern pieces.

The colors that have been used in the diagrams are suggestions only. Remember, a design can look completely different simply by changing fabric texture, color, and print.

Before Beginning

Gathering Tools

The following is a list of the most commonly used tools for quilting and appliquéing, and hints on when and how they should be used. Be sure to read the manufacturer's instructions carefully before beginning a project and take care to follow those directions exactly.

Hand-stitching may be done on all projects that require sewing, but sometimes a sewing machine makes it easier and quicker when adding borders, hanging straps, mitering corners, or making yo-yos.

Marking Tools

Test the marking tool on the fabric first to make certain the marks can be removed easily. Always use a light hand when marking with any marking tool.

To mark around cardboard templates on light-colored fabrics, use a sharp #2 lead pencil. On dark-colored fabrics, use a sharp white dressmaker's pencil, a sliver of soap, or a silver or yellow fabric marking pencil. Chalk pencils or chalk-wheel markers also make clear marks on fabric. Also, disappearing ink pens may be used when marking.

Needles

Needles come in many sizes and lengths. When purchasing needles, remember that the larger the number, the finer the needle. Having a variety of needles on hand is recommended.

Sharps are fine, strong needles with round eyes. They are good for mending and hand-sewing.

Embroidery or crewel needles are sharp needles with long, oval eyes. They are used to stitch fine to medium surfaces. Common sizes are 1 to 10.

Darning needles are long, strong needles with large eyes. They are good for basting and work best when stitching with heavy threads. Keep an assortment of sizes 14 to 18.

Betweens are round-eyed needles, but are shorter than sharps. Common sizes are 5 to 12.

Chenille needles are long-eyed needles with a sharp point. They are good for stitching with heavy threads. Common sizes are 18 to 24.

Scissors & Pinking Shears

Fabric scissors are used for cutting fabric and should be designated for that purpose only. Using fabric scissors to cut other materials will dull the blades and make them less effective.

Craft scissors are essential for cutting cardboard, paper, and plastic templates. They are very strong and have a very refined cutting edge, which makes it possible to get into tight areas.

Embroidery scissors are generally only used for cutting threads.

Pinking shears have notched or serrated blades. They are used to cut edges of fabric with a zig-zag pattern for decorative purposes and are often used to prevent edges of fabric from fraying.

Choosing Fabrics, Threads & Battings

The following is a list of the most commonly used fabrics, threads, and battings for quilting and appliquéing and hints on when and how they should be used:

Fabrics

Fabrics will need to be selected for backing, for backgrounds, and for each motif. The texture, color, and print of fabrics to be used should depend on the desired look of the finished project, as well as the skill of the crafter. Each fabric chosen should be appropriate for the use of the finished project — a piece that needs to be laundered frequently should not be made from non-washable fabrics. Also, keep in mind how easily a particular fabric frays. A fabric that frays very easily will be hard to work with and the edges will have to be secured in some way. Raw edges can generally be cut with pinking shears to prevent fraying.

Quilting fabrics include calico, muslin, and broadcloths. They are medium-weight fabrics made from 100% cotton. Calico and other printed fabrics are available in a variety of patterns and colors. Muslin is white or off-white and is usually used for the background in a pieced design. Broadcloth is a plain weave fabric and is generally a solid color.

Threads

The considerations for fabric choice also apply to thread choice. The type of thread used should be appropriate for the style and use of the finished piece. Another consideration in choosing thread is the type of fabric(s) being used. Like threads should go with like fabrics — natural threads with natural fabrics and synthetic threads with synthetic fabrics.

Embroidery threads of all kind can be used. The color and character of thread are usually subservient to the fabric used, but not always. Sometimes contrasting stitching adds as much to the design as the material itself.

Battings

Batting is used as the middle layer of a quilt. Bonded cotton batting gives a flat, natural appearance and comes in different thicknesses. Polyester batting gives a puffy appearance. Felt may be substituted and renders the same appearance as the bonded cotton batting.

Preparing Fabrics

Before marking and/or cutting, make certain the fabrics have been laundered, dried, and pressed. If the finished piece will be laundered, make certain the fabrics used are preshrunk and colorfast.

Basic Construction

Enlarging Motif Pattern Pieces & Placement Diagrams

All patterns are a reduction of the original size unless specified otherwise. Enlarge patterns to the indicated percentage using a photocopy machine. It is best to use a professional copy center.

If it is desired that the finished project be larger or smaller than the one photographed, adjust enlargements or reductions as needed.

Tracing Motif Pattern Pieces & Placement Diagrams onto Tracing Paper

Lay a sheet of tracing paper on top of enlarged motif pattern pieces and placement diagram. Trace the designs to make a template or full-scale outlined drawing for all pattern pieces.

Preparing & Cutting Out Motifs

When cutting out motifs, be certain to add seam allowances when necessary. Always cut out on a flat surface so fabrics do not pucker.

Preparing Motifs for Hand-Sewing

Mark and pin the traced designs on the motif fabrics. Then cut out allowing a small margin around the traced lines.

Preparing Motifs with Fusible Web

1. Trace pattern from book.

2. Enlarge as necessary.

3. Trace pattern onto translucent tracing paper.

4. Turn tracing paper over so pattern is visible in reverse.

5. Place fusible web on top of reverse pattern, paper side up.

6. Trace pattern on paper side of fusible web.

7. Cut out pattern on fusible web leaving a ¼" border around pattern.

8. Follow manufacturer's instructions to fuse the fusible web to the motif fabrics.

9. Cut out pattern following pattern line.

10. Fuse the fabric motifs to project.

Preparing Motifs with Double-Sided Adhesive

Always pre-test double-sided adhesive on fabrics to be used. Peel off paper backing (printed side). Apply sticky side on wrong side of fabrics. Trace patterns on paper backing and cut out motifs on the traced lines.

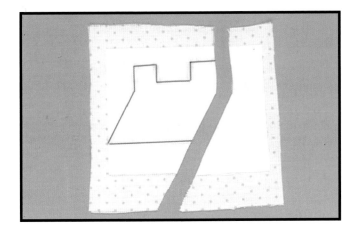

Tracing Placement Diagram onto Background Fabric

Tracing using Tracing Paper

Using the full-sized placement diagrams for positioning, pin the traced placement diagrams to the background fabric. Pin or baste along the traced lines. Tear the tracing paper away. This method is not as accurate as tracing the design directly onto the fabric using transfer paper.

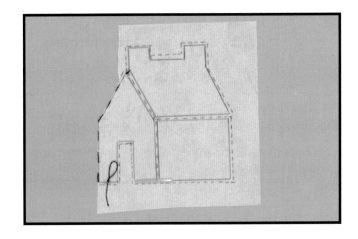

Tracing using Transfer Paper

Since transfer paper comes in many colors, choose a paper that is closest in color and tone to the background fabric being used. However, it must be able to be seen. Be certain to follow the manufacturer's instructions. To reduce the amount of marks on the fabric, trace with dashed lines instead of solid lines.

Place the traced placement diagram to the background fabric and pin it in place. Insert a piece of transfer paper between the diagram and the fabric. Trace over diagram, transferring marks to fabric.

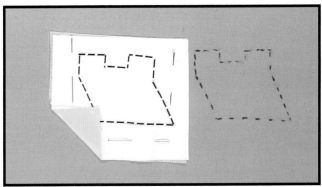

Attaching Motifs

When the design has been transferred to the background, simply place the motifs over the marked outlines.

Attaching Motifs for Hand-Sewing

Hand-stitch motifs as indicated in the assembly instructions for each project.

Attaching Motifs with Fusible Web

Fuse motifs to background fabrics following manufacturer's instructions.

Attaching Motifs with Double-Sided Adhesive

Adhere motifs to background fabrics following manufacturer's instructions.

Layering & Stitching

After cutting the backing and batting, create a "quilt sandwich" in three layers in the following order: backing, batting, and assembled quilt top.

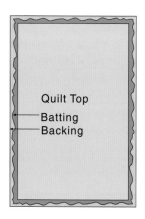

First, lay the backing, wrong side up, on a clean, flat surface. Be careful not to stretch the backing out of shape. Next, lay the batting on top of the backing, smoothing out all wrinkles. Last, lay the assembled quilt top on top of the batting, right side up. Smooth out any wrinkles.

If necessary, pin or baste in place. Finish the mini quilt by stitching around the edges. Use stitches as indicated in the assembly instructions for each project or as desired.

Finishing

Mitering Corners

Lay the first corner to be mitered on the ironing board. Fold under one strip at a 45° angle and adjust so seam lines match perfectly. Press and pin securely.

Fold the fabric diagonally with right sides together, lining up the edges of the border. If necessary, use a ruler to draw a pencil line on the creases to make the line more visible.

Stitch on the pressed crease, sewing from the corner to the outside edge. Press the seam open and trim away excess border strip, leaving a ¼"-wide seam allowance. Repeat for the three remaining corners.

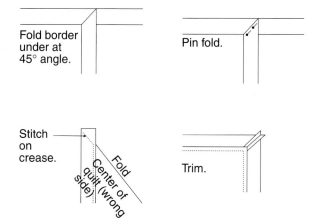

Making Borders

Cutting directions are given for the border strips in the assembly instructions for each project.

Fold long edges of backing over edges of assembled quilt top. Turn under ½", pin in place, and blindstitch. Repeat process for short edges. When all four sides have been blindstitched, press border flat.

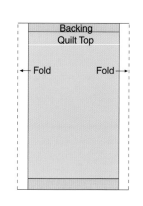

Adding A Hanging Strap

A hanging strap must be added if the mini quilt is to be hung. This strap will hold the hanger, whether it be a wooden dowel, a twig, or a cinnamon stick.

Use desired scraps of fabric and cut as indicated in the assembly instructions for each project. Fold the fabric straps in half, wrong sides together. Attach these straps to the back of the project as indicated.

Adding Decorative Accents

Decorative accents range from buttons and beads to charms and personal items. Buttons and beads can be sewn on in the traditional manner. Charms and other objects can be secured in place with fabric or craft glue.

Outline stitching is also considered a decorative accent and should be done with a permanent ink pen. Be careful not to leave the pen on fabric too long or it will run.

Making Yo-Yos

Yo-Yos are the circular-shaped decorative fabric accents that embellish many of the projects in this book. They are often used to replicate flowers.

Cut out a circle in the appropriate size for each yo-yo. A ¼" seam allowance has already been added.

Stitch a gathering stitch ¼" along the circumference of each circle. Draw up the circle and tuck the raw edges into the center of the yo-yo. Press flat with the gathering in the center.

Additional Techniques

Blush Painting

Using a round fabric-dye brush and acrylic paint, dip brush in paint and blot off excess paint onto a paper towel. Very lightly "blush" desired areas.

Gathering

Gathering refers to machine- or hand-stitching two parallel rows of long stitches ¼" to ½" from edge of fabric. Leave ends of thread 2" or 3" long. Pull the two threads and gather fabric to fit required measurement. Long edges may need to be gathered from both ends. Disperse fullness evenly and secure the threads. A heavy thread is recommended; be careful to avoid breaking the threads.

Painting on Fabric

Painting on fabric requires the use of a textile medium. To use a textile medium, pour a small amount of paint onto a palette. Place a few drops of textile medium on the paint. Mix it into the paint. The paint will become more transparent as more textile medium is added.

After the patterns have been traced onto the fabrics, paint in the background colors first. Then, go back and paint the details. It will be similar to coloring in a coloring book — be certain to stay within the traced lines.

Allow the paint to dry thoroughly. Most fabrics painted with textile medium can be heat-set in a dryer or with a warm iron on the reverse side of the fabric.

There are several brands to choose from, but the manufacturer's instructions must be followed for the brand that is being used.

Sponge Painting

Dip a small damp sponge into paint and blot off excess onto a paper towel. Blot the surface of the project, using light or heavy coverage as desired.

Stenciling

Transfer patterns onto a piece of clear acetate or a piece of lightweight cardboard. Use a craft knife or single-edged razor to cut out the portion of the design to be stenciled from the acetate or cardboard. Secure the stencil in place with masking tape.

Load the stencil brush with stencil paint and blot off excess on a paper towel. Too much paint left on the stencil brush will cause the paint to seep underneath the stencil. Bounce the stencil brush up and down across the open portion of the stencil. Remove the stencil and fill in any unwanted spaces.

Embroidery Stitches

Back Stitch

Bring needle up at A; go down at B to the right of A. Come back up at C to the left of A. Repeat B-C, inserting the needle in the same hole.

Blanket Stitch

Similar to the buttonhole stitch, but the stitches are farther apart.

Blind or Slip Stitch

Insert needle in folded edge of fabric for the length of the stitch (⅛" to ¼"). Bring it out and take small stitch through second piece of fabric.

Buttonhole Stitch

Bring needle up at A; go down at B. Bring needle up again at C keeping thread under the needle. For second stitch, go down at D and back up at E.

French Knots

Bring needle up through fabric at A. Smoothly wrap floss around the needle once. Hold floss securely off to one side, push the needle down through the fabric at B.

Herringbone Stitch

Work the stitch from right to left. Bring needle up at A; go down at B. Bring needle up again at C taking a small horizontal backstitch. Continue working, alternating from side to side.

Lazy Daisy Stitch

Bring needle up at A and form a loop. Go down at B as close to A as possible, but not into A. Come up at C and bring the tip of the needle over the thread. Go down at D, making a small anchor stitch.

Running or Whip Stitch

A line of straight stitches with an unstitched area between each stitch. Bring needle up at A; go down at B.

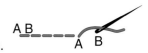

Satin Stitch

Bring needle up at A; go down at B forming a straight stitch. Bring needle up again at C and go down again at D forming another smooth straight stitch that slightly overlaps the first straight stitch. Repeat to fill the design area.

Stem Stitch

Working from left to right, make slightly slanting stitches along the designated line. Bring needle up at A then insert needle through fabric at B. Bring needle back up at C, which is at the midpoint of the previous stitch. Make all stitches the same length. Insert needle through fabric at D and continue on in the same manner.

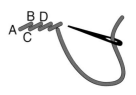

Straight Stitch

Bring needle up at A; go down at B forming a straight stitch the desired length.

"X" or Cross Stitch

Bring needle up at A; go down at B forming a straight stitch the desired length. Cross the stitch with an equal-sized stitch coming up at C and going down at D.

Definitions

Acrylic: Acrylic or water-based paints work best for fabric painting because they dry quickly and come in a variety of pre-mixed colors. They clean up easily with soap and water when still wet.

Appliqué: The art of applying fabric cutouts or other materials to a background to create a decorative pattern.

Background: Material to which motifs are applied.

Backing: The fabric that forms the bottom or back layer of a quilt.

Basting Stitches: Long running stitches used to hold two or more layers of fabric in place temporarily. To be removed when quilting is finished.

Batting: Layers or sheets of cotton or polyester material used as a filler between the quilt top and the backing.

Border: Plain, pieced, or appliquéd bands of fabric, used to frame the central section of the quilt top.

Crazy Quilting: A piecing technique using small, irregularly shaped pieces of fabric and decorative stitches.

Decorative Stitch: A stitch used to decorate an appliqué design as opposed to a stitch used to secure the motif in place.

Double-sided Adhesive: No-sew, no-iron material used to secure fabric to backing or background fabric.

Fusible Web: Often used to secure a motif to a background before stitching. A web with weak adhesive can easily be removed if desired. Different webs are made for different types of fabric.

Hand-stitched Method: Hand-stitching motifs to a background.

Layering: To create a "quilt sandwich" with three layers: backing, batting, and assembled quilt top.

Machine-stitched Method: Machine-stitching motifs to a background. Good for heavy fabrics that are difficult to hand-stitch or for items that will be used heavily or laundered frequently. Has a sharper appearance than hand-stitched appliqué.

Mitering a Corner: Joining vertical and horizontal strips of fabric at a 45° angle to form a 90° corner.

Mixed-media Appliqué: Use of other materials in combination with fabric to create a design. Can also refer to the use of dying and hand-painting techniques in combination with appliqué.

Motif: A piece of the appliqué design.

Motif Patterns: Pattern pieces to be traced onto tracing paper, then cut out and traced onto motif or background fabrics.

Placement Diagram: A reference drawing of the finished appliqué. It can also be used as a pattern.

Quilting: Sewing layers of fabric and batting together by hand or by using a sewing machine. It is often decorative and is generally the finishing step in appliqué or piecing.

Seam Allowance: The distance between the cut edge of fabric and the stitching line. In quilts, this is usually ¼". However, if the pieces of the quilt are small, ¼" seam allowances may overlap on the back when the quilt is assembled, causing excess bulk. If this occurs, trim seam allowances to ⅛".

Textile Medium: A necessary paint additive used when painting on fabrics. It prevents paints from peeling and helps to permanently adhere them to fabrics.

Tracing Paper: A relatively transparent paper used to trace patterns and placement diagrams.

Transfer Paper: A paper coated on one side with graphite or chalk. When it is pressed by a pencil, it transfers the graphite or chalk to the surface underneath it.

Joy Stocking

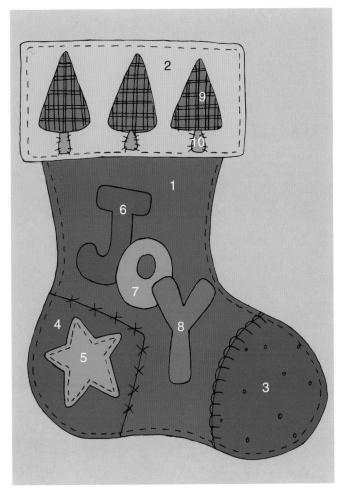

Placement Diagram
Enlarge 200%

General Instructions

Basic Construction—pages 10–13
Embroidery Stitches—page 14

Assembly

1. Trace, apply fusible web to, and cut out pieces 1–10 according to General Instructions. See additional pattern pieces on page 36.

2. Cut out batting and backing using pinking shears, ¼" larger than piece 1.

3. Fuse piece 1 to batting piece 1, following manufacturer's instructions. Fuse piece 2 to piece 1. Fuse pieces 3–4 and 6–8 to piece 1. Fuse piece 5 to piece 4. Fuse pieces 9–10 to piece 2. See Placement Diagram.

4. Layer batting and assembled background. Pin. Sew a running stitch to stitch layers together.

5. Buttonhole-stitch along inside edge of piece 3. Sew large "X"-stitches along inside edge of piece 4. Make straight-stitches along outer edges of piece 10.

6. Tie three bows across top of stocking using thread and attach decorative mini hanger to the back for hanging.

7. If using light colored fabrics for pieces 5–8, outline stitches using a permanent ink pen.

Materials

Fabric: assorted for motifs
    backing: 7" x 9"
Cotton batting: thin bonded, 7" x 9"
Fusible web
Iron and ironing board
Needles
Straight pins
Thread: coordinating
Permanent ink pen
Scissors
Pinking shears
Tracing paper and marking tool
Decorative mini hanger

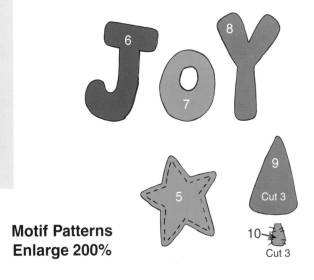

Motif Patterns
Enlarge 200%

18 Debra Crabtree-Lewis

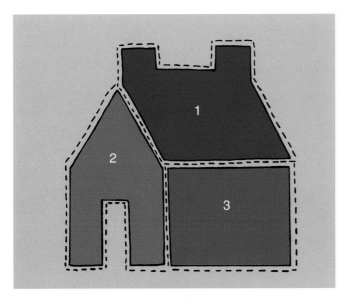

Placement Diagram
Enlarge 200%

Materials

Fabric: assorted cottons for motifs and borders
    background: 8¼" x 6¼"
    outside borders: 3½" x 16½" (2); 4½" x 6½" (2)
Cotton batting: thin bonded, 8" x 10"
Fusible web
Iron and ironing board
Straight pins
Thread: coordinating
Sponge
Acrylic paint: desired color
Permanent ink pen
Sandpaper
Scissors
Sewing machine
Tracing paper and marking tool
Frame: pine, 8" x 10"
Cardboard: 7½" x 9½"
Masking tape

Stenciled House

General Instructions

Basic Construction—pages 10–13
Additional Techniques—page 13

Assembly
¼" seam allowance

1. Sponge-paint frame. Let paint dry thoroughly. Sand edges of frame slightly to distress.

2. Trace, apply fusible web to, and cut out pieces 1–3 according to General Instructions.

3. Pin and sew side borders to background. Pin and sew top and bottom borders to background. See photograph.

4. Fuse pieces 1–3 to background. See Placement Diagram.

5. Outline stitches along border of background and pieces 1–3 using a permanent ink pen.

6. Place assembled quilt top right side down. Place batting on top. Place cardboard on top of batting. Wrap edges of quilt around cardboard. Tape to secure. Mount and secure in frame.

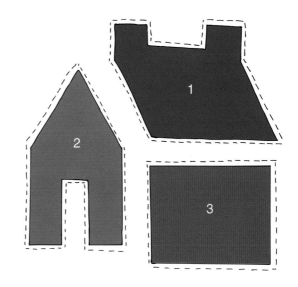

Motif Patterns
Enlarge 200%

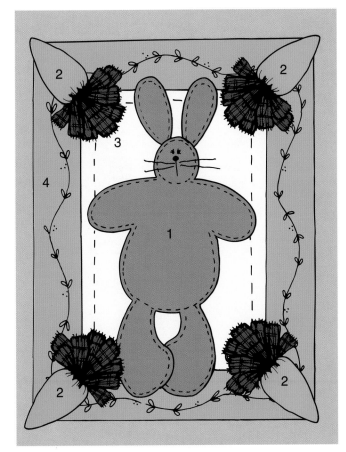

Placement Diagram
Enlarge 200%

Materials

Fabric: assorted cottons for motifs
    backing: 11" x 9"
    piece 3 (center): 6½" x 4½"
    piece 4 (background): 9" x 7"
    carrot tops: 2" x ⅜" (16)
    bunny's dress: 6" x 2"
Cotton batting: ¼" thick, 9" x 7"; thin, 6½" x 4½"
Fusible web
Iron and ironing board
Needles
Straight pins
Thread: coordinating
Embroidery floss: coordinating
Stuffing: polyester
Paintbrush: round fabric-dye, #4
Acrylic paint: blush-color
Textile medium
Permanent ink pen
Scissors
Sewing machine
Tracing paper and marking tool

Carrot & Bunny

General Instructions

Basic Construction—pages 10–13
Additional Techniques—page 13
Embroidery Stitches—page 14

Assembly

¼" seam allowance

1. Trace, apply fusible web to, and cut out piece 1 according to General Instructions. See pattern pieces on page 36.

2. Cut out four of piece 2.

3. Layer backing, thick batting, and background. Pin. Fold backing over edges of piece 4. Fold ½" under, pin to front. Do longer sides first. Blind-stitch. Fold top and bottom edges ½" under, pin to front. Blind-stitch. Press.

4. Center thin batting and piece 3 on piece 4. Straight-stitch thin batting and piece 3 to piece 4, ¼" from edge. Do not stitch through backing fabric.

5. Fuse piece 1 to pieces 3 and 4, following manufacturer's instructions. See Placement Diagram.

6. With wrong sides together, sew side seam of piece 2, using ¼" seam allowance. Trim seams to ⅛" and trim tip. Turn right side out. Repeat for remaining three carrots.

7. Gather-stitch ¼" from top edge of each carrot. Stuff lightly with stuffing. Gather threads. Tuck raw edges inside carrot and knot off.

8. Cut fabric for carrot tops. Gather four pieces of fabric for each carrot top. Straight-stitch to top center of each carrot. See Diagram A on page 36.

9. Outline vine border on piece 4 using a permanent ink pen. Outline stitches and facial details on front of quilt.

10. Gather-stitch fabric for bunny's dress. Draw up gathers. Sew dress on bunny's body and sew assembled carrots to each corner of quilt top. See photograph.

11. Using paintbrush, lightly blush bunny's cheeks, ears, hands, and feet with blush-color acrylic paint.

12. Hang as desired.

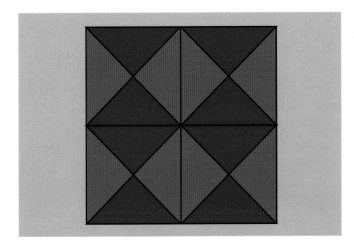

Placement Diagram

Materials

Fabric:
    polished cotton squares: 4" x 4" (8)
    polished cotton squares to coordinate
      with first cotton squares: 4" x 4" (8)
    polished cotton for backing: 9" square
    polished cotton for ruffle: 84" x 3½"
Needles
Straight pins
Thread: coordinating
Stuffing: polyester
Scissors
Iron and ironing board
Sewing machine

Patchwork Pillow

General Instructions

Basic Construction—pages 10–13
Additional Techniques—page 13
Embroidery Stitches—page 14

Assembly
¼" seam allowance

1. When cutting squares, cut so each square is exactly 4" x 4".

2. Fold each square in half diagonally. Press flat.

3. Pillow top is assembled in quarter sections. Begin with piece 1, Diagram A. Lay piece 2 on piece 1. Sew along stitch lines in Diagram B. Lay piece 3 on piece 2. Sew along stitch lines in Diagram C. Lay piece 4 on piece 3. Sew along stitch lines in Diagram D. Tuck piece 4 under piece 1. Stitch along last edge, Diagram E.

4. After each quarter section is complete, sew together as a four patch. Alternate colors so center looks like a pinwheel. See Placement Diagram.

5. Cut out ruffle fabric. Make a ⅛" finished hem on one long edge. Gather-stitch other long edge. Sew short edges of ruffle together.

6. Place quilt front, right side up. Place ruffle right side down on quilt fabric with hemmed edge on inside. Adjust gathers to fit. Stitch ruffle to quilt front. Place backing fabric on top of quilt front and ruffle, right side down. Stitch all three layers together on three sides. Turn right side out. Stuff. Blind-stitch opening closed.

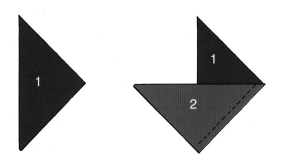

Diagram A   Diagram B

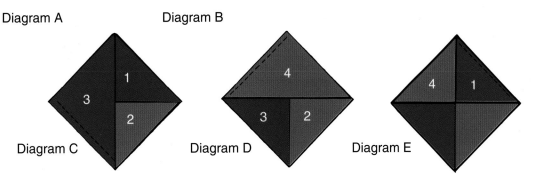

Diagram C   Diagram D   Diagram E

**Placement Diagram
Enlarge 200%**

Materials

Fabric: assorted cottons for motifs
    backing: 11" x 9",
    background: 9" x 7"
    piece 1: muslin, 6" x 6"
Cotton batting: thin bonded, 9" x 7"
Fusible web
Iron and ironing board
Needles
Straight pins
Thread: coordinating
Embroidery floss: coordinating
Permanent ink pen
Buttons: wood, ⅜"-diameter (2)
Scissors
Tracing paper and marking tool

**Motif Patterns
Enlarge 200%**

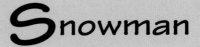

Snowman

General Instructions

Basic Construction—pages 10–13
Embroidery Stitches—page 14

Assembly

1. Trace, apply fusible web to, and cut out pieces 1–10 according to General Instructions. Fuse pieces 1–10 to background, following manufacturer's instructions. Sew wood buttons to vest using thread. See Placement Diagram.

2. Layer backing, batting, and assembled background. Pin. Fold backing borders to front of assembled quilt. Miter corners. Secure corners with a stitch in each corner. See photograph.

3. Buttonhole-stitch around the borders of assembled quilt.

4. Outline stitches around snowman's body, nose, bottom of vest, heart, and patch using a permanent ink pen. Make dots for snowman's eyes using a permanent ink pen.

5. Hang as desired.

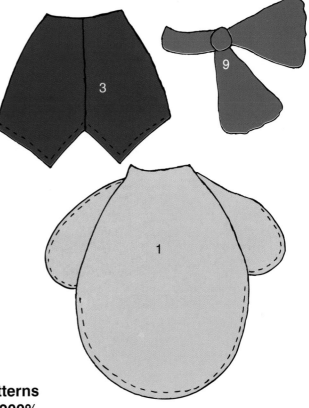

Debra Crabtree-Lewis 25

Placement Diagram
Enlarge 250%

Materials

Fabric: assorted cottons for motifs
    backing: 9" x 7"
    spools: broadcloth, 8" x 10"
    center patch: muslin, 6¼" x 4½"
    outside borders: 1½" x 4½" (2); 1½" x 6¼" (2)
    squares for outside borders: 1½" x 1½" (4)
Cotton batting: thin bonded, 9" x 7"
Fusible web
Iron and ironing board
Needles
Straight pins
Thread: neutral-colored
Embroidery floss: coordinating
Permanent ink pen
Scissors
Pinking shears
Sewing machine
Tracing paper and marking tool

▌Love Quilts

General Instructions

Basic Construction—pages 10–13
Embroidery Stitches—page 14

Assembly
¼" seam allowance

1. Sew one square border piece to each end of 6¼" border strips, right sides together.

2. Sew two 4½" border strips to center patch. Press. Pin and sew together top and bottom border pieces to center patch, making certain corners match. Press seams and top.

3. Trace, apply fusible web to, and cut out pieces 1–4 according to General Instructions. Fuse pieces 1, 3, and 4 to background and piece 2 to piece 1, following manufacturer's instructions. Buttonhole-stitch around piece 3. Straight-stitch around piece 4. See Placement Diagram.

4. Outline stitches on assembled quilt and spools using a permanent ink pen.

5. Layer backing, batting, and assembled background. Pin. Straight-stitch layers together. Trim edges with pinking shears.

6. Make one large and one small yo-yo (pieces 5 and 6). Sew on center patch. Tie bows using neutral-colored thread and sew to front of each yo-yo. See photograph.

7. Hang as desired.

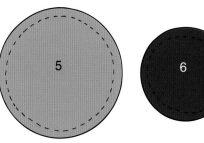

Yo-Yo Patterns
Enlarge 200%

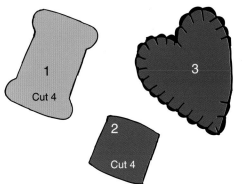

Motif Patterns
Enlarge 200%

28 Debra Crabtree-Lewis

Placement Diagram
Enlarge 200%

Materials

Fabric: assorted cottons for motifs
    backing: 9" x 7"
    background: 9" x 7"
Cotton batting: thin bonded, 9" x 7"
Fusible web
Iron and ironing board
Needles
Straight pins
Thread: coordinating
Permanent ink pen
Scissors
Pinking shears
Tracing paper and marking tool

Basket of Posies

General Instructions

Basic Construction—pages 10–13
Embroidery Stitches—page 14

Assembly
¼" seam allowance

1. Trace, apply fusible web to, and cut out pieces 1–5 according to General Instructions.

2. Fuse pieces 1–5 to background, following manufacturer's instructions. Fuse them in the following order: piece 1, piece 5, pieces 4, pieces 2, and pieces 3. See Placement Diagram.

3. Outline stitches around pieces 1, 2, 4, and 5 using a permanent ink pen. See photograph.

4. Layer backing, batting, and assembled background. Pin. Straight-stitch layers together. Trim edges with pinking shears.

5. Hang as desired.

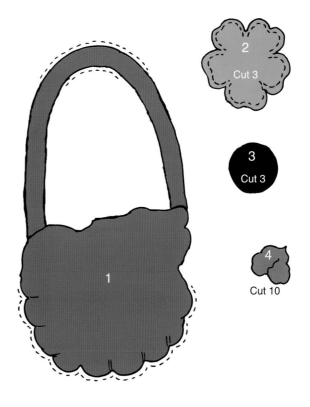

Motif Patterns
Enlarge 200%

**Placement Diagram
Enlarge 255%**

Materials

Fabric: assorted cottons for motifs
  backing: 8" x 10"
  background: 7" x 9"
Cotton batting: thin bonded, 7" x 9"
Fusible web
Iron and ironing board
Needles
Straight pins
Thread: neutral-colored
Pencil
Permanent ink pen
Buttons: medium (3)
Scissors
Tracing paper and marking tool

In the Garden

General Instructions

Basic Construction—pages 10–13
Embroidery Stitches—page 14

Assembly

1. Trace, apply fusible web to, and cut out pieces 1–3 according to General Instructions.

2. Fuse pieces 1–3 to background, following manufacturer's instructions. See Placement Diagram.

3. Make three yo-yos (piece 4). Stitch yo-yos in place on background. Stitch buttons to center of yo-yos.

4. Outline stitches around pieces 1–3 and stems using a permanent ink pen.

5. Trace lettering with a pencil. Outline lettering using a permanent ink pen. See Lettering Diagram.

6. Tie bow to handle of piece 1 using neutral-colored thread.

7. Layer backing, batting, and assembled background. Pin. Fold backing to front of quilt. Blind-stitch.

8. Hang as desired.

**Lettering Diagram
Enlarge 200%**

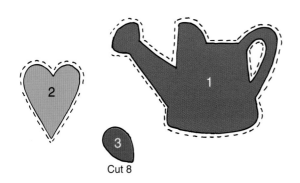

Cut 8

**Motif Patterns
Enlarge 200%**

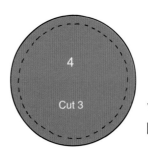

Cut 3

**Yo-Yo Pattern
Enlarge 200%**

Debra Crabtree-Lewis

Placement Diagram
Enlarge 270%

Materials

Fabric: assorted cottons for motifs
    backing: muslin, 8" x 7"
    background: muslin, 8" x 7"
Cotton batting: thin bonded, 8" x 7"
Fusible web
Iron and ironing board
Needles
Straight pins
Thread: coordinating
Permanent ink pen
Scissors
Pinking shears
Tracing paper and marking tool

Watering Can

General Instructions

Basic Construction—pages 10–13
Embroidery Stitches—page 14

Assembly

1. Trace, apply fusible web to, and cut out pieces 1–6 according to General Instructions.

2. Fuse pieces 1–6 to background, following manufacturer's instructions. See Placement Diagram.

3. Layer backing, batting, and assembled background. Pin. Straight-stitch layers together. Trim edges with pinking shears.

4. Make four large and four small yo-yos (pieces 7 and 8). Stitch large yo-yos on background. Stitch small yo-yos to center of large yo-yos.

5. Outline stitches, bee's wings, and antennas using a permanent ink pen.

6. Hang as desired.

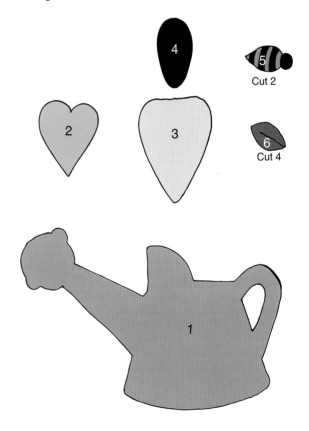

Motif Patterns
Enlarge 200%

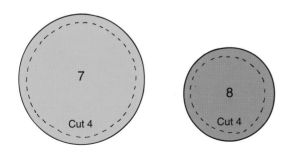

Yo-Yo Patterns
Enlarge 200%

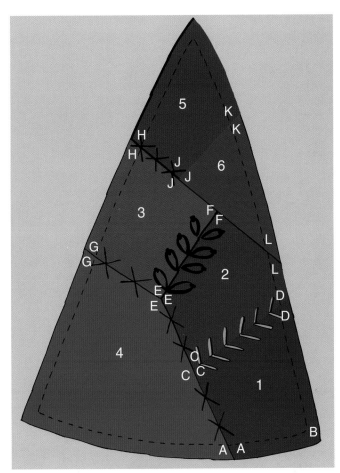

Placement Diagram
Enlarge 200%

Materials

Fabric: assorted for pieces
   backing: 6½" x 8½"
Needles
Straight pins
Thread: coordinating
Embroidery floss: coordinating
Stuffing: polyester
Paintbrush
Acrylic paint: desired color
Dowel: wooden, ⅜"-diameter, 10"
Tassel
Spanish moss
Styrofoam ball: 2"-diameter
Terra cotta pot: 3"
Hot glue gun and glue sticks
Iron and ironing board
Precision ruler
Scissors
Pinking shears
Old scissors or knife
Sewing machine
Tracing paper and marking tool

Christmas Tree

General Instructions

Basic Construction—pages 10–13
Embroidery Stitches—page 14

Assembly
¼" seam allowance

1. Cut out pieces 1–7 and backing fabric. See pattern pieces on page 36.

2. Crazy-quilt pieces, right sides together. Sew pieces 1–2 from points C to D. Sew pieces 2–3 from points E to F. Sew pieces 1–4 from points A to G. Sew pieces 5–6 from points J to K. Sew pieces 5–6 from points H to L. Press seams open on backside. See Placement Diagram.

3. Stem-stitch pieces 2–3 from points E to F. Lazy daisy-stitch along sides of stem stitch. Cross-stitch pieces 1–4 from points A to G. Cross-stitch piece 3 and 5 from points H to J. Straight-stitch, angling to look like a zipper, pieces 1–2 from points C to D.

4. Pin and sew together front piece to back piece, wrong sides together. Leave an opening at bottom center for stuffing and dowel. Press. Trim edges with pinking shears for "pine tree" edge. Stuff tree.

5. Pin and sew star, wrong sides together. Clip a small opening in back of star for stuffing. Clip edges with pinking shears. Stuff points first with small pea size balls of stuffing. Stuff remainder of star tightly. Whip-stitch back opening closed. Make long, straight stitches from center of star to outside. Make three French knots in center of star. Hot-glue star to top of tree.

6. To cut dowel, place precision ruler on dowel at desired breaking point, score all the way around dowel with old scissors or knife. Break by placing scored line on square-edge of table or counter. Put pressure on end until it snaps. Insert dowel into tree. Close up opening on tree bottom with hot glue. Paint dowel and terra cotta pot. Hot-glue styrofoam ball into bottom of pot. Insert tree into pot. Cover styrofoam ball with Spanish moss. Tie tassel to dowel.

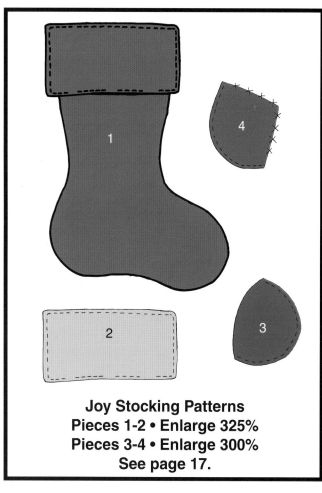

Joy Stocking Patterns
Pieces 1-2 • Enlarge 325%
Pieces 3-4 • Enlarge 300%
See page 17.

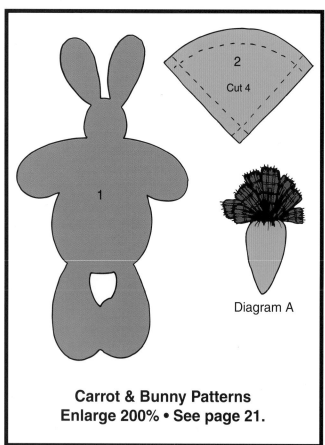

Diagram A

Carrot & Bunny Patterns
Enlarge 200% • See page 21.

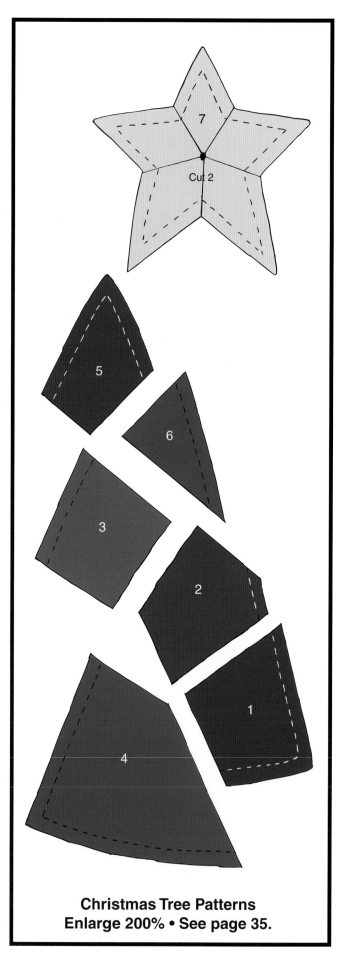

Christmas Tree Patterns
Enlarge 200% • See page 35.

Birdhouses For Rent Pattern

Welcome Home Pattern

Garden Vegetable Patches Pattern

Pansy Pot Pattern

Cherry Pie Patch Pattern

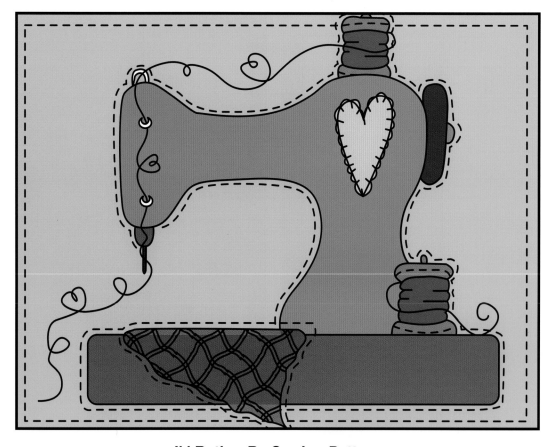

I'd Rather Be Sewing Pattern

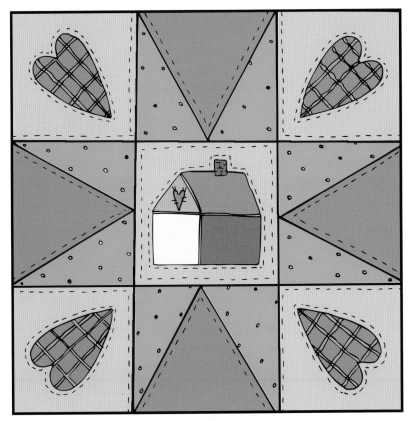

Traditional Star Pattern

Country Patch Patterns

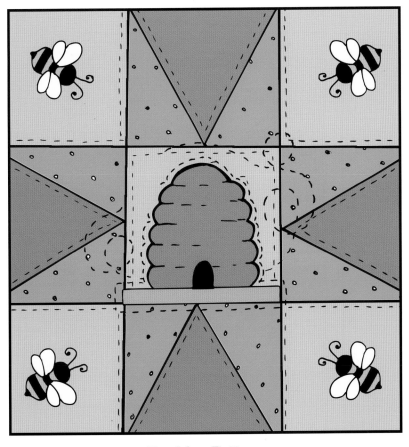

Beehive Pattern

**Pumpkin
Patch
Pattern**

Country Santa Pattern

Winter Patches Pattern

Summer Garden Pattern

Garden Gatherings Pattern

Gardening Angel Pattern

I Believe In Angels Pattern

Teddy Bear Repair Pattern

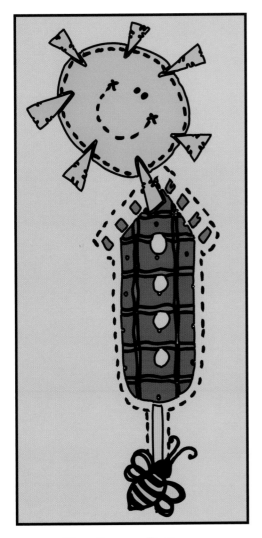

Bee House Pattern

Patchwork Rooster Pattern

Watermelon Pattern

**Placement Diagram
Enlarge 270%**

Materials

Fabric:
  background: 8" x 9½"
  patch behind piece 1: muslin, 4" x 4"
  patch behind piece 2: muslin, 4" x 3"
  patch behind piece 3: muslin, 4" x 4½"
  patch behind piece 4: muslin, 4" x 5½"
  patch behind piece 5: muslin, 8" x 1½"
Cotton batting: thin bonded, 8" x 9½"
Needles
Straight pins
Embroidery floss: coordinating
Stencil brushes
Stencil paints: desired colors
Masking tape
Clear acetate or lightweight cardboard
Pencil
Permanent ink pens: #8; #3
Pinking shears
Craft knife
Tracing paper and marking tool

A Time And A Season

General Instructions

Basic Construction—pages 10–13
Additional Techniques—page 13
Embroidery Stitches—page 14

Assembly

1. Cut out background, muslin patches, and batting using pinking shears.

2. Very lightly trace motif patterns onto appropriate muslin patches using a pencil. See Placement Diagram.

3. Paint designs on muslin patches. Several coats of paint may be needed. Allow paint to dry between coats.

4. Trace lettering with a pencil. Outline lettering using a #8 permanent ink pen. See Lettering Diagram on page 63. Outline stitches around muslin patches using a #3 permanent ink pen.

5. Pin painted muslin patches to background. Place batting behind background. Straight-stitch layers together.

6. Hang as desired.

**Motif Patterns
Enlarge 200%**

**Placement Diagram
Enlarge 250%**

General Instructions

Basic Construction—pages 10-13
Additional Techniques—page 13
Embroidery Stitches—page 14

Assembly

1. Cut out batting using pinking shears. Apply double-sided adhesive to batting.

2. Trace and apply fusible web to background, borders, and pieces 1–9 according to General Instructions. Cut out pieces 1–12. See additional pattern pieces on page 63.

3. Pin and fuse background to batting, following manufacturer's instructions. Fuse borders around background. Fuse pieces 1–9 to background. See Placement Diagram.

4. Make five large (piece 10), three medium (piece 11) and three small (piece 12) yo-yos. Glue two large yo-yos to assembled quilt.

5. Straight-stitch stem from large yo-yo to heart on hat.

6. Adhere batting to canvas bag. Glue remaining yo-yos to canvas bag. See photograph.

Materials

Fabric: assorted for motifs
    background: 7" x 9"
    outside borders: 1" x 8" (2); 1" x 9½" (2)
Cotton batting: thin bonded, 8" x 9½"
Fusible web
Iron and ironing board
Needles
Straight pins
Thread: coordinating
Double-sided adhesive
Glue: fabric
Scissors
Pinking shears
Tracing paper and marking tool
Canvas bag

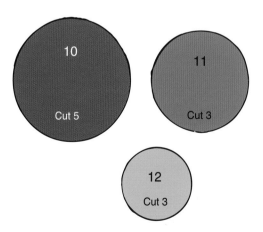

**Yo-Yo Patterns
Enlarge 200%**

Kathy Distefano-Griffiths

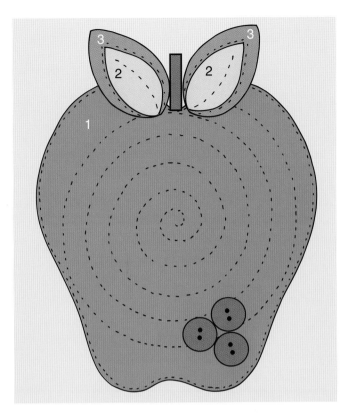

Placement Diagram
Enlarge 250%

Materials

Fabric: assorted for motifs
    background: 10½" x 10½"
Cotton batting: thin bonded, 8" x 14";
    scraps for piece 3
Polyester batting: thin bonded, 10" x 10"
Fusible web
Iron and ironing board
Needles
Straight pins
Thread: heavy, coordinating
Cinnamon stick: 4"
Buttons: medium (3)
Glue: fabric
Scissors
Pinking shears
Tracing paper and marking tool
Pillow: 14"

Apple Pillow

General Instructions

Basic Construction—pages 10–13
Embroidery Stitches—page 14

Assembly

1. Apply fusible web to background. Trim to 10" x 10" using pinking shears.

2. Cut out piece 1 using pinking shears. Cut out cotton batting ¼" larger than piece 1. Trace quilting lines on front side of apple with marking tool. Pin apple to top of batting. Quilt, following traced quilting lines, using heavy thread. See additional pattern piece and quilting lines on page 63.

3. Cut out four of piece 3 using pinking shears and apply fusible web. Cut out two cotton batting pieces ¼" larger than piece 3. Layer one cotton batting leaf between two large leaves. Pin. Straight-stitch layers together using heavy thread. Repeat for second leaf. See Placement Diagram.

4. Trace, apply fusible web to, and cut out two of piece 2 according to General Instructions. Fuse one small leaf to the front of each large leaf, following manufacturer's instructions.

5. Sew three buttons to front of quilted apple.

6. Cut polyester batting ½" smaller than piece 1. Apply fabric glue to back edges of assembled piece 1. Lay polyester batting in the center of background. Lay quilted apple in center of background. Insert 4" cinnamon stick at top of apple. Press edges to secure glue.

7. Glue bottom edges of assembled leaves to apple, at the sides of the cinnamon stick.

8. Attach to 14" pillow.

Motif Patterns
Enlarge 200%

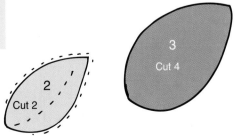

Kathy Distefano-Griffiths 49

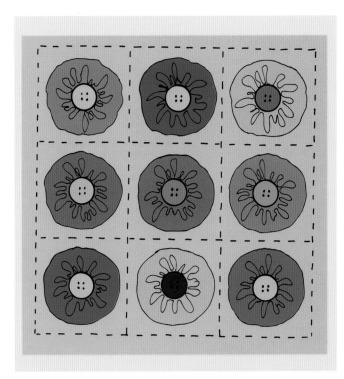

**Placement Diagram
Enlarge 200%**

Materials

Fabric: assorted flannel prints and plaids
    background: muslin, 8" x 8"
Cotton batting: thin bonded, 8" x 8"
Buttons: small (9)
Needles
Straight pins
Embroidery floss: coordinating
Linen jute or small natural cording
Disappearing ink pen
Glue: fabric
Ruler
Scissors
Tracing paper and marking tool
Frame: wooden, with 7" opening
Foam mounting board
Masking tape

Nine-Square Yo-Yo

General Instructions

Basic Construction—pages 10–13
Embroidery Stitches—page 14

Assembly

1. Using a ruler and a disappearing ink pen, measure and mark a 6" square in middle of background. Divide into nine 2" squares.

2. Pin background to batting. Sew a running stitch to form a pattern of nine 2" squares. Remove pins. See Placement Diagram.

3. Make yo-yos. *Note: Flannel fabric is thicker than regular cotton fabric so the centers will not draw up small and tight. However, the buttons will cover the openings.* Glue a yo-yo in the center of each 2" square.

4. Sew buttons to yo-yo centers using linen jute or small natural cording.

5. Place assembled quilt top right side down. Place mounting board on top of batting. Tape to secure. Mount and secure in frame.

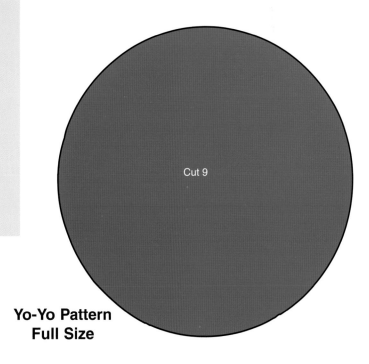

Cut 9

**Yo-Yo Pattern
Full Size**

Kathy Distefano-Griffiths

**Placement Diagram
Enlarge 245%**

Materials

Fabric: assorted cottons for motifs
    background: 6½" x 8"
    outside borders: ¾" x 7¼" (1); ¾" x 8¾" (2)
    straps: 1" x 3" (2)
Cotton batting: thin bonded, 8" x 9½";
    scraps for piece 1
Stuffing: cotton
Fusible web
Iron and ironing board
Needles
Straight pins
Thread: coordinating
Embroidery floss: coordinating
Linen jute or small natural cording
Paintbrush
Acrylic paint: desired color
Blush makeup
Buttons: ½"-diameter, assorted (5)
Snaps: (2)
Glue: fabric and wood
Scissors
Pinking shears
Tracing paper and marking tool
Dowel: wooden, ⅜"-diameter, 9"
Spools: wooden, to fit wooden dowel (2)

Stuffed Snowman

General Instructions

Basic Construction—pages 10–13
Embroidery Stitches—page 14

Assembly

1. Cut out pieces 1 and 14 from batting using pinking shears. Cut out background and batting using pinking shears. See pattern pieces on page 64.

2. Trace, apply fusible web to, and cut out pieces 2–13 and 15 according to General Instructions.

3. Fray edges of borders. Pin and straight-stitch borders to background using linen jute or small natural cording.

4. Fuse pieces 2–7 to piece 1, following manufacturer's instructions.

5. Pin and straight-stitch piece 1 to background. Leave a small opening at bottom end to stuff snowman's body. Insert stuffing. Straight-stitch bottom end opening closed and straight-stitch snowman's mouth.

6. Fuse pieces 8–13 to background. Randomly straight-stitch around snowman's heart. See Placement Diagram.

7. Fuse piece 15 to piece 14. Glue pieces to front of quilt. See Placement Diagram.

8. Sew buttons to tree and birdhouse. Sew buttons in top corners.

9. Glue snaps on snowman's face for eyes.

10. Apply blush makeup to snowman's cheeks.

11. Tear two straps. Fold straps over and sew to each corner on back side of batting for hanging.

12. Paint dowel and spools. Let paint dry thoroughly. Using wood glue, adhere spools to ends of dowel and thread dowel through quilt straps.

54 Kathy Distefano-Griffiths

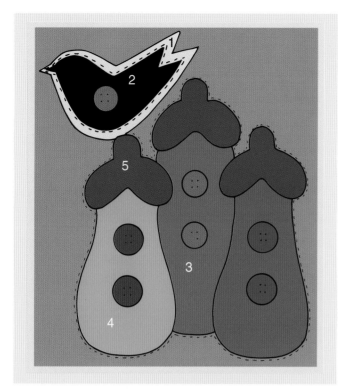

**Placement Diagram
Enlarge 275%**

Materials

Fabric: assorted cottons for motifs
    background: 7" x 8½"
Cotton batting: thin bonded, 8" x 9½";
    piece 1
Fusible web
Iron and ironing board
Needles
Straight pins
Embroidery floss: coordinating
Linen jute or small natural cording
Buttons: ¾"- to 1¼"-diameter (7)
Permanent ink pen
Scissors
Pinking shears
Tracing paper and marking tool
Twigs
2-ply jute

Harvest Pumpkin

General Instructions

Basic Construction—pages 10–13
Embroidery Stitches—page 14

Assembly

1. Cut out batting for piece 1. Cut out background using pinking shears. Apply fusible web to background. See additional pattern pieces on page 63.

2. Trace, apply fusible web to, and cut out pieces 2–5 according to General Instructions. Fuse background to batting, following manufacturer's instructions.

3. Fuse pieces 3–5 to background. Fuse piece 2 to piece 1.

4. Straight-stitch around quilt next to background. See photograph.

5. Pin and straight-stitch assembled pieces 1–2 to background.

6. Sew buttons to crow and pumpkins using linen jute or small natural cording.

7. Outline stitch around pumpkins and pumpkin tops using a permanent ink pen. See Placement Diagram.

8. Using 2-ply jute, tie two loops for hanging. Sew to back of quilt and thread twigs through the loops.

9. Hang as desired.

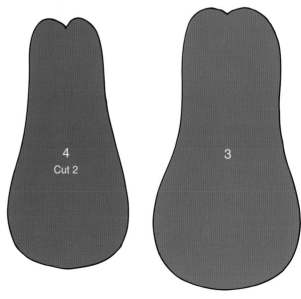

**Motif Patterns
Enlarge 200%**

Kathy Distefano-Griffiths

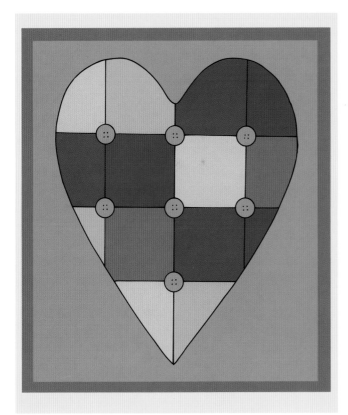

Placement Diagram
Enlarge 270%

Materials

Fabric:
    assorted flannel squares: 2½" x 2½" (14)
    background: 9" x 10¾"
    outside borders: 2½" x 11" (2); 2½" x 15" (2)
Cotton batting: thin bonded, 9" x 10¾"
Fusible web
Iron and ironing board
Needles
Straight pins
Embroidery floss: coordinating
Linen jute or small natural cording
Buttons: small (7)
Scissors
Tracing paper and marking tool
Sewing machine
Glue: fabric

Patchwork Heart

General Instructions

Basic Construction—pages 10–13
Embroidery Stitches—page 14

Assembly
¼" seam allowance

1. Arrange and sew flannel squares together. Cut out heart shape from assembled squares. See Placement Diagram for pattern to cut out heart shape.

2. Apply fusible web to background. Center and fuse background to batting, following manufacturer's instructions.

3. Pin assembled heart to center of background. Blanket-stitch around edge of heart. See photograph.

4. Sew longer border strips to sides of background, using ½" seam allowance. If necessary, trim ends of strips. Sew shorter border strips to top and bottom of background. Fold the top and bottom to back side of quilt. Tuck raw edges under batting and glue to secure.

5. Sew buttons to corners of each square using linen jute or small natural cording.

6. Hang as desired.

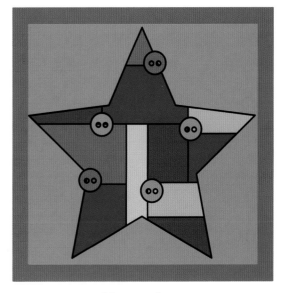

Alternative
Patchwork Design

Kathy Distefano-Griffiths 57

Kathy Distefano-Griffiths

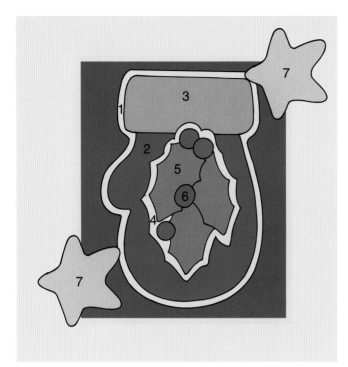

Placement Diagram
Enlarge 250%

Materials

Fabric: assorted cottons for motifs
    background: felt, 6" x 8¾"
    pieces 2 and 7: felt
    straps: felt, 1⅛" x 4" (2)
    sleeve: 2" x 45"
Cotton batting: thin bonded, 6¼" x 9";
    pieces 1 and 4
Fusible web
Iron and ironing board
Needles
Straight pins
Thread: coordinating
Embroidery floss: coordinating
Paintbrush
Acrylic paint: desired color
Pine garland
Cinnamon sticks
Glue: fabric
Scissors
Pinking shears
Sewing machine
Tracing paper and marking tool
Dowel: wooden, ⅜"-diameter, 24"
Beads: wooden, to fit wooden dowel (2)

Mitten Banner

General Instructions

Basic Construction—pages 10–13
Additional Techniques—page 13
Embroidery Stitches—page 14

Assembly

1. Cut out background and piece 7 using pinking shears. Cut out pieces 1 and 4 from batting using pinking shears. See additional pattern pieces on page 65.

2. Trace, apply fusible web to, and cut out pieces 2–3 and 5–6 according to General Instructions.

3. Fuse pieces 2–3 to piece 1, following manufacturer's instructions. Fuse pieces 5–6 to piece 4. See Placement Diagram.

4. Layer batting and background. Pin. Straight-stitch layers together.

5. Glue piece 4 to piece 2. Glue piece 1 around the edges to background, leaving top edge of cuff open.

6. Sew a running stitch around each star. Glue stars to background.

7. Fold straps over and sew to each corner on back side of batting for hanging.

8. Sew a sleeve and turn it right side out.

9. Paint dowel and beads. Let paint dry thoroughly. Place fabric sleeve over dowel and gather. Using wood glue, adhere beads to ends of dowel and thread dowel through quilt straps. *Note: The length of this dowel should be altered if only one of the three banners is to be hung.*

10. Fill mitten with pine garland and cinnamon sticks.

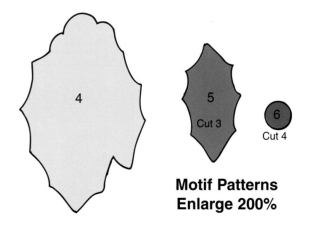

Motif Patterns
Enlarge 200%

**Placement Diagram
Enlarge 250%**

Materials

Fabric: assorted cottons for motifs
   background: felt, 6" x 8¾"
   pieces 3 and 10: felt
   straps: felt 1⅛" x 4" (2)
Cotton batting: thin bonded, 6¼" x 9";
   pieces 1–2
Fusible web
Iron and ironing board
Needles
Straight pins
Thread: coordinating
Embroidery floss: coordinating
Pine garland
Cinnamon sticks
Glue: fabric
Scissors
Pinking shears
Tracing paper and marking tool

Stocking Banner

General Instructions

Basic Construction—pages 10–13
Embroidery Stitches—page 14

Assembly

1. Cut out background and piece 10 using pinking shears. Cut out pieces 1–2 from batting using pinking shears. See additional pattern pieces on page 65.

2. Trace, apply fusible web to, and cut out pieces 3–10 according to General Instructions.

3. Fuse pieces 4–6 to piece 3, following manufacturer's instructions. Fuse pieces 7–9 to piece 2. See Placement Diagram.

4. Layer batting and background. Pin. Straight-stitch layers together.

5. Glue assembled tree to pieces 3–4. Glue piece 1 around the edges to background, leaving top edge of cuff open.

6. Sew a running stitch around each star. Glue stars to background.

7. Fold straps over and sew to each corner on back side of batting for hanging. See instructions for making hanger on page 60, steps 8–9.

8. Fill stocking with pine garland and cinnamon sticks.

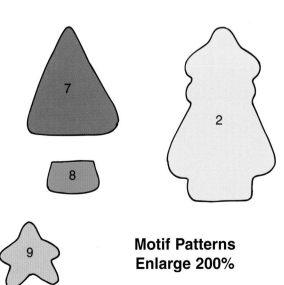

**Motif Patterns
Enlarge 200%**

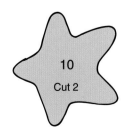

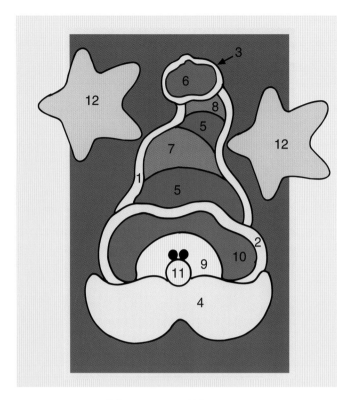

Placement Diagram
Enlarge 200%

Materials

Fabric: assorted cottons for motifs
    background: felt, 6" x 8¾"
    pieces 5 and 12: felt
    pieces 9 and 11: felt, flesh color
    straps: felt, 1⅛" x 4" (2)
Cotton batting: thin bonded, 6¼" x 9";
    enough to stuff piece 11;
    beard strands, ½" x 8" (30);
    pieces 1–4
Fusible web
Iron and ironing board
Needles
Straight pins
Thread: coordinating
Embroidery floss: coordinating
Blush makeup
Snaps: (2)
Glue: fabric
Scissors
Pinking shears
Tracing paper and marking tool

Santa Banner

General Instructions

Basic Construction—pages 10–13
Additional Techniques—page 13
Embroidery Stitches—page 14

Assembly

1. Cut out background and piece 12 using pinking shears. Cut out pieces 1–4 from batting using pinking shears. See pattern pieces on page 66.

2. Trace and apply fusible web to pieces 5–10 according to General Instructions. Cut out pieces 6–8 and 10. Cut out pieces 5, 9, and 11 from felt.

3. Fuse pieces 7–8 to piece 5, following manufacturer's instructions. Fuse piece 5 to piece 1. Fuse piece 6 to piece 3. Fuse piece 3 to piece 1. Fuse piece 9–10 to piece 2. Fuse piece 2 to piece 1. See Placement Diagram.

4. Layer batting and background. Pin. Straight-stitch layers together.

5. Glue piece 1 to background.

6. Gather-stitch edges of piece 11. Insert cotton batting inside of nose. Draw up tightly and secure threads.

7. Cut out beard strands from batting using pinking shears. Sew a gathering stitch across top of beard to connect all strands. Draw up beard to fit Santa's face. Glue beard and nose to Santa's face. Randomly tie knots in 15 beard strands. If necessary, trim ends.

8. Sew a running stitch around the two mustaches (piece 4). Glue mustache on top of beard.

9. Glue snaps to Santa's face for eyes.

10. Sew a running stitch around each star. Glue stars to background.

11. Apply blush makeup to Santa's cheeks and nose.

12. Fold straps over and attach to each corner on back side of batting for hanging. See instructions for making hanger on page 60, steps 8–9.

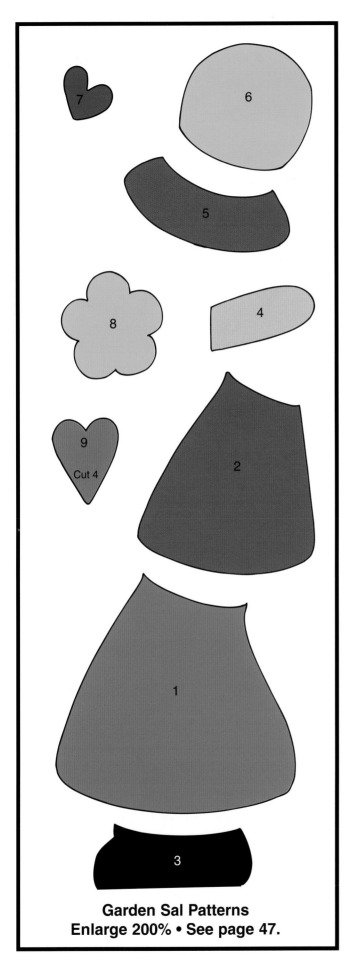

Garden Sal Patterns
Enlarge 200% • See page 47.

Lettering Diagram
Enlarge 200% • See page 45.

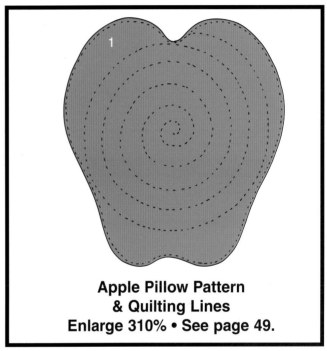

Apple Pillow Pattern
& Quilting Lines
Enlarge 310% • See page 49.

Harvest Pumpkin Patterns
Enlarge 200% • See page 55.

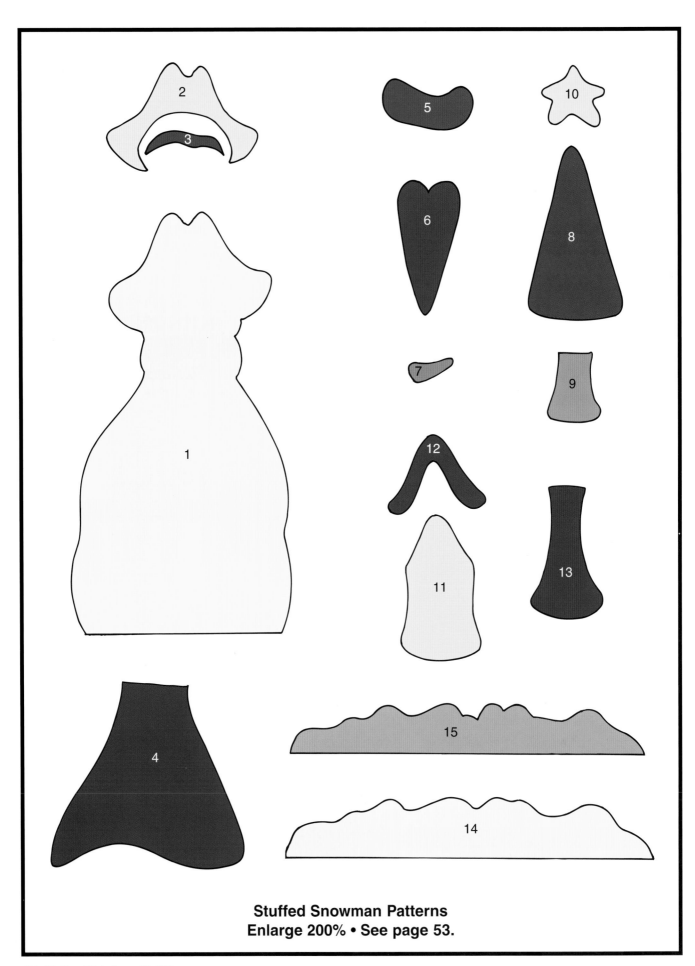

Stuffed Snowman Patterns
Enlarge 200% • See page 53.

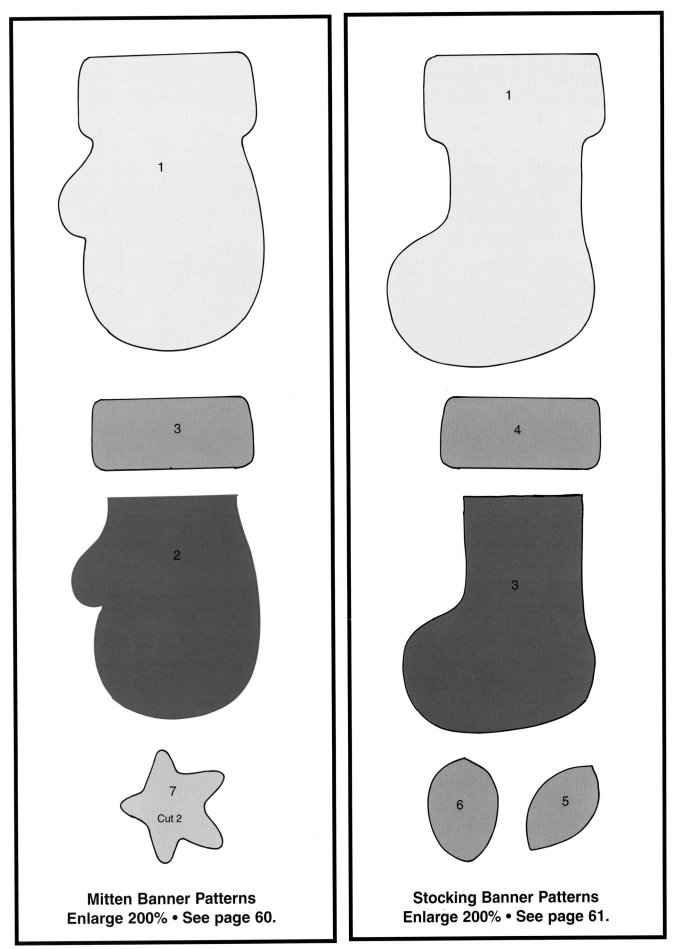

Mitten Banner Patterns
Enlarge 200% • See page 60.

Stocking Banner Patterns
Enlarge 200% • See page 61.

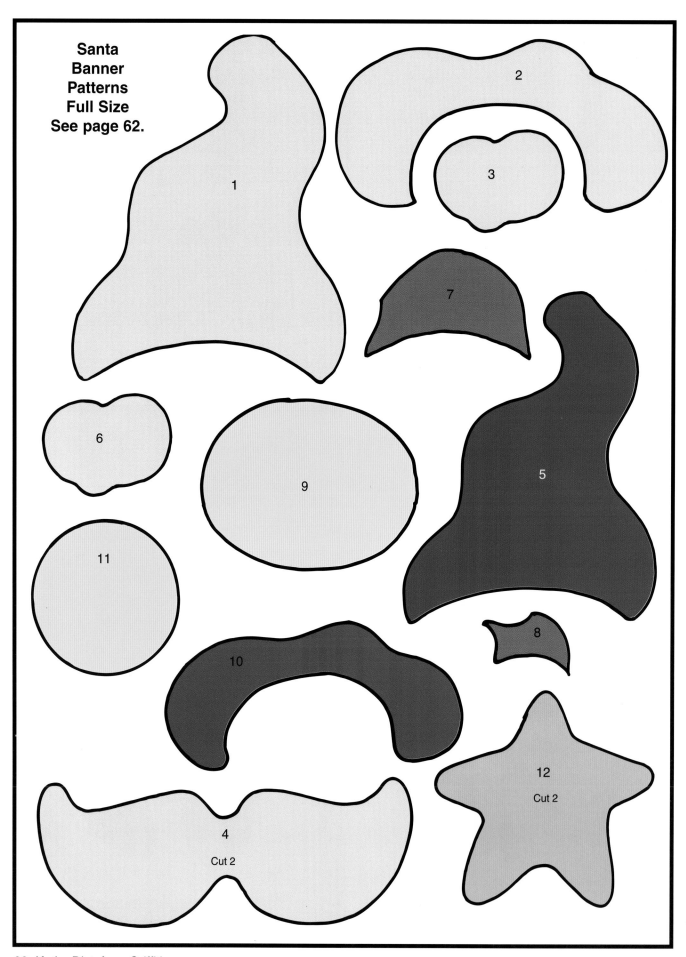

**Santa
Banner
Patterns
Full Size
See page 62.**

1

2

3

7

6

9

5

11

8

10

4

Cut 2

12

Cut 2

Welcome Pattern

Happy Home Pattern

Good Day Pattern

Henny Penny Pattern

Sunny Sunflowers Pattern

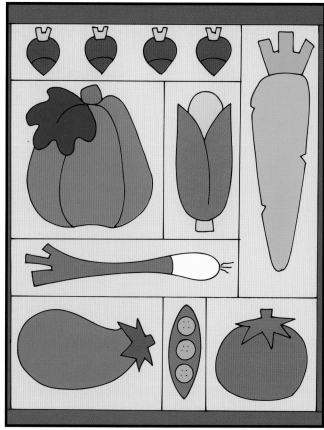

Veggie Patchwork Pattern

Country Garden Squares Pattern

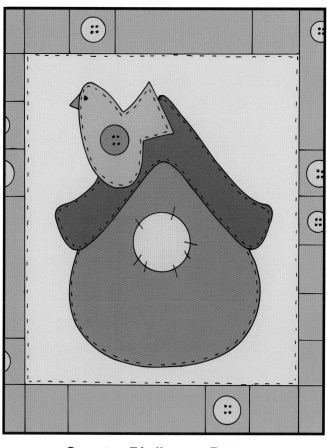

Country Birdhouse Pattern

We Love Cats Pattern

Bird on Birdhouse Pattern

Grandpa's Barn Pattern

Flowers In Pot Pattern

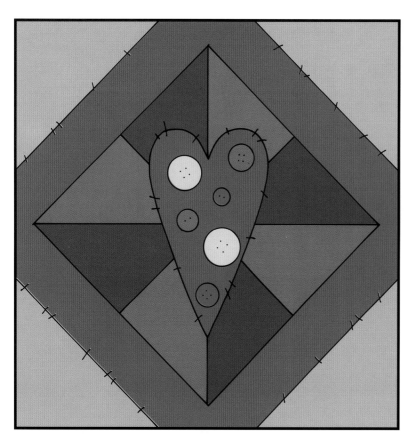

Heart Patchwork Pattern

Beehive Pattern

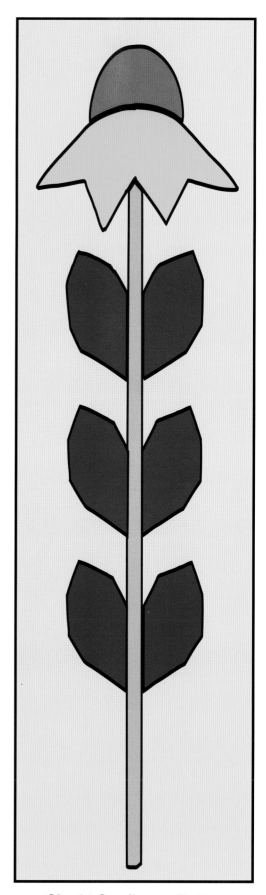

Single Sunflower Pattern

Pine Tree Retreat Pattern

Canes, Trees & Stockings Pattern

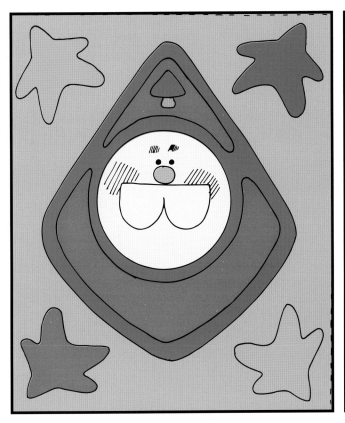

Stenciled Santa Pattern

Angels Pattern

72 Emily Dinsdale

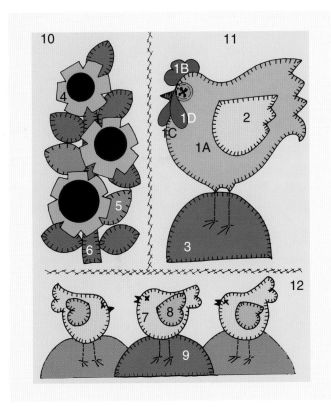

Placement Diagram
Enlarge 230%

Materials

Fabric: assorted cottons for motifs
    piece 10: 7½" x 4¼";
    piece 11: 7¼" x 5¼";
    piece 12: 4" x 9"
    backing: 12" x 13½"
Cotton batting: thin bonded, 10¾"x 9¼"
Fusible web
Iron and ironing board
Needles
Straight pins
Thread: coordinating
Embroidery floss: coordinating
Buttons: assorted sizes
Scissors
Sewing machine
Tracing paper and marking tool

Hen & Chicks

General Instructions

Basic Construction—pages 10–13
Embroidery Stitches—page 14

Assembly
¼" seam allowance

1. Sew pieces 10–12 together.

2. Trace, apply fusible web to, and cut out pieces 1–9 according to General Instructions. See additional pattern pieces on page 92.

3. Fuse pieces 1–9 to pieces 10–12, following manufacturer's instructions. See Placement Diagram.

4. Herringbone-stitch seams between pieces 10–11 and where piece 12 connects to pieces 10–11.

5. Blanket-stitch around edges of pieces 1A–3, 5–8, and middle hill only.

6. Cross-stitch chicks' eyes. Satin-stitch hen's beak and chicks' beaks. Straight-stitch hen's and chicks' legs.

7. Sew buttons to flower centers. Sew button on for hen's eye.

8. Layer backing, batting, and assembled quilt. Pin. Fold backing to front of quilt and buttonhole-stitch around edges.

9. Hang as desired.

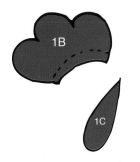

Motif Patterns
Full Size

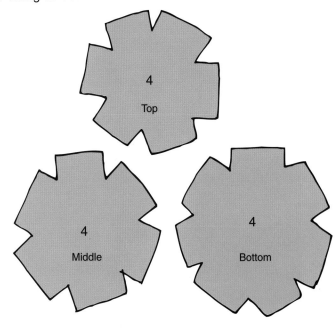

**Placement Diagram
Enlarge 260%**

Buttercup

General Instructions

Basic Construction—pages 10–13
Embroidery Stitches—page 14

Assembly

1. Cut out background, backing, batting, and patches using pinking shears.

2. Trace and apply fusible web to pieces 1–14 according to General Instructions. Cut out pieces 1–16.

3. Straight-stitch patches to background. Layer backing, batting, and background. Pin. Straight-stitch layers together. Trim with pinking shears.

4. Fuse pieces 1–14 to patches, following manufacturer's instructions. See Placement Diagram.

5. Straight-stitch pieces 15–16 to assembled quilt.

6. Make four yo-yos (piece 17) and glue to quilt.

7. Cross-stitch cow's eyes.

8. Tie knot in end of twine and glue in place for cow's tail.

9. Tie a bow from fabric strip and glue to front of milk bottle.

10. Hang as desired.

Materials

Fabric: assorted cottons for motifs
    backing: 11" x 7½"
    background: 11" x 7½"
    patch behind cow: fabric and felt, 5½" x 5"
    patch behind milk bottle:
        fabric and felt, 2¾" x 5½"
    bow: 10" x 1"
Cotton batting: thin bonded, 11" x 7½"
Fusible web
Iron and ironing board
Needles
Straight pins
Embroidery floss: coordinating
Twine: 4"
Glue: fabric
Scissors
Pinking shears
Tracing paper and marking tool

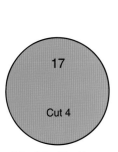

**Yo-Yo Pattern
Enlarge 200%**

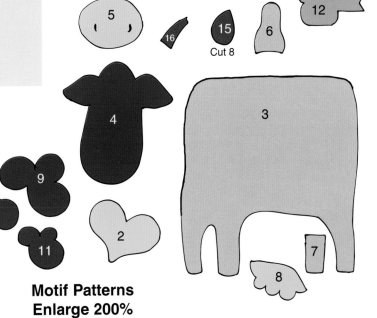

**Motif Patterns
Enlarge 200%**

Emily Dinsdale 75

Placement Diagram
Enlarge 230%

Materials

Fabric: assorted felt for motifs
    backing: felt, 8¾" x 10"
    background: felt, 8¾" x 10"
    center patch: fabric and white felt, 6½" x 8"
    piece 1: flannel and white felt; 2" x 2" (4 each)
Cotton batting: 8¾" x 10"
Stuffing: polyester
Needles
Straight pins
Embroidery floss: coordinating
Pencil
Permanent ink pen
Ribbon: ¼"-wide, 6" (2)
Buttons: small (2); medium (2); large (4)
Bead: small (1)
Glue: fabric
Scissors
Pinking shears
Tracing paper and marking tool

Stuffed Bear

General Instructions

Basic Construction—pages 10–13
Embroidery Stitches—page 14

Assembly

1. Cut out backing, batting, background, four flannel and four white felt for piece 1, using pinking shears. See pattern pieces on page 92.

2. Fray edges of center patch fabric. Cut out felt for pieces 2–7.

3. Trace lettering with a pencil. Outline lettering using a permanent ink pen. See Lettering Diagram.

4. Layer backing, batting, and background. Pin. Straight-stitch layers together. Straight-stitch center patch and white felt to background. See Placement Diagram.

5. Place and pin pieces 2–7 to center patch. Stuff bear's tummy and head. Straight-stitch around edges of pieces 2–7 on center patch.

6. Straight-stitch center of bear's tummy, legs, arms, and head. Make an "X"-stitch for the bear's belly button. Add random stitches crossing over each other on bottoms of paws and on ears.

7. Sew two small buttons on bear's face for eyes. Sew one medium button on an arm and one on a leg. Glue on small bead for bear's nose. Straight-stitch around bear's muzzle. Lazy daisy-stitch bear's mouth.

8. Stitch ribbons to sides of bear's neck. Tie in a bow and trim excess.

9. Pin pieces 1 (flannel and white felt) to assembled quilt in each corner. Attach by sewing button in center of each corner patch.

10. Hang as desired.

Lettering Diagram
Enlarge 210%

Please don't feed the

Placement Diagram
Enlarge 235%

Materials

Fabric: assorted cottons for motifs
    backing: off-white felt, 8½" x 8"
    background: 8½" x 8"
Fusible web
Iron and ironing board
Needles
Straight pins
Thread: coordinating
Embroidery floss: coordinating
Buttons: small (4)
Glue: craft
Scissors
Tracing paper and marking tool
Decorative wooden bee

Honeycomb

General Instructions

Basic Construction—pages 10–13
Embroidery Stitches—page 14

Assembly

1. Trace and apply fusible web to piece 1 according to General Instructions. Cut out pieces 1–3.

2. Fuse honeycomb pieces to background, following manufacturer's instructions. See Placement Diagram.

3. Straight-stitch around honeycomb. See photograph.

4. Straight-stitch leaves to background.

5. Make four yo-yos (piece 3) and sew to corners of background.

6. Sew button to center of each yo-yo.

7. Layer backing and assembled quilt. Pin. Straight-stitch layers together.

8. Glue wooden bee to quilt.

9. Hang as desired.

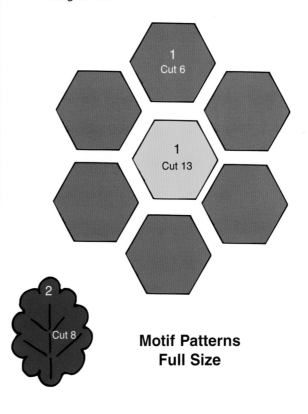

Motif Patterns
Full Size

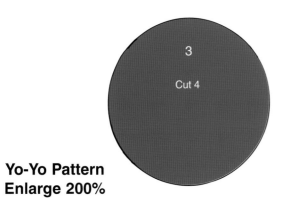

Yo-Yo Pattern
Enlarge 200%

Bunny Book Cover

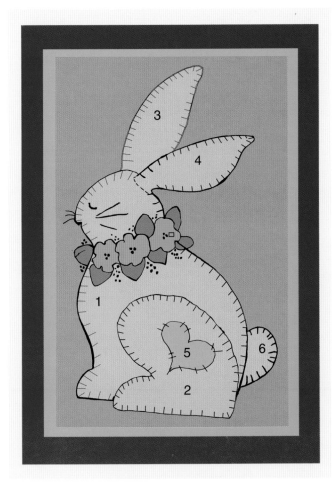

Placement Diagram
Enlarge 200%

Materials

Fabric: assorted felt for motifs
    bottom background: pink felt, 6" x 7¾"
    top background: beige felt, 6¼" x 8"
    book cover: green felt, measure to fit
Needles
Straight pins
Thread: coordinating
Embroidery floss: coordinating
Blush makeup
Ribbon: pink ¾"-wide, 30";
    green ¾"-wide, 7"
Beads: ⅜"-diameter gold (9);
    ⅛"-diameter pink (40)
Scissors
Pinking shears
Ruler

General Instructions

Basic Construction—pages 10–13
Additional Techniques—page 13
Embroidery Stitches—page 14

Assembly

1. Cut out both backgrounds using pinking shears. See pattern pieces on page 93.

2. Measure the book to be covered. Add ¾" to its length and 4" to its width. Cut out felt for book cover using pinking shears. Fold ends in 2" on front and back. Pin. Straight-stitch along top and bottom edges of book cover. See Diagram A on page 93.

3. Layer backgrounds and batting. Place on book cover. Straight-stitch layers together around background edges. Place an "X"-stitch in each corner. See photograph.

4. Cut out pieces 1–6.

5. Layer both felt pieces 1–3 and 6. Blanket-stitch pieces 1–3 and 6, going through both layers, to background. Blanket-stitch piece 4 to background. Straight-stitch piece 5 to piece 2. See Placement Diagram.

6. Cut green ribbon into seven 1"-long pieces. Fold ribbon to form a point. Sew ribbon leaves around bunny's neck.

7. Cut pink ribbon into three 4"-long pieces. Sew a gathering stitch along one side of each pink ribbon. Gather threads to form a circle. Attach in center of leaves.

8. Cut remaining pink ribbon into two 9"-long pieces. Sew one ribbon to front of book cover and one ribbon to back side of book cover. Tie a bow on the front.

9. Sew three gold beads in center of each ribbon flower. Sew pink beads on the bunny around the flowers.

10. Apply blush makeup to bunny's cheeks and ears.

Emily Dinsdale

**Placement Diagram
Enlarge 135%**

Materials

Fabric: assorted cottons for motifs
   backing: 5½" x 7"
   background: 4½" x 6"
Cotton batting: thin bonded, 4½" x 6"
Needles
Straight pins
Embroidery floss: coordinating

Ripe Apple

General Instructions

Basic Construction—pages 10–13
Embroidery Stitches—page 14

Assembly

1. Cut out pieces 1–2 and backing using pinking shears.

2. Straight-stitch edge of piece 1 to background using linen jute. Sew button on piece 1. Straight-stitch leaves to background down the center. See Placement Diagram.

3. Sew 2½" twig with an "X"-stitch for apple stem on top of the apple and between the two leaves.

4. Layer backing, batting, and assembled quilt. Pin. Fold backing to front of quilt and herringbone-stitch layers together.

5. Sew a button to each corner of assembled quilt.

6. Tie remaining twig to top of quilt using cording for hanging.

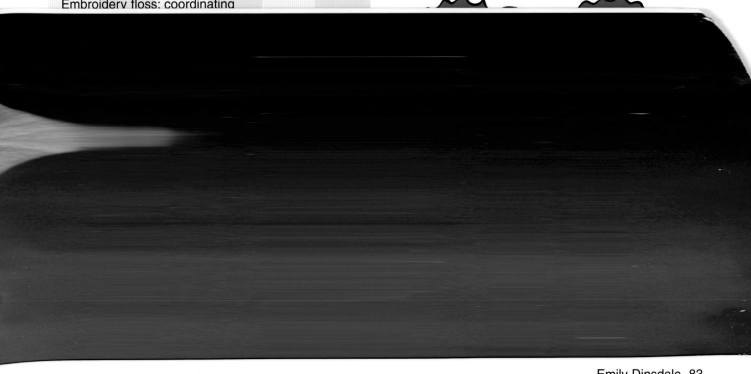

84 Emily Dinsdale

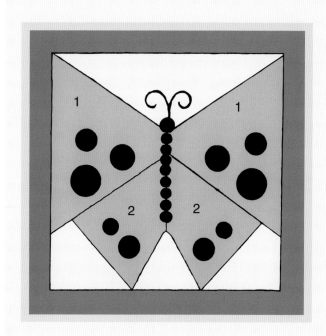

**Placement Diagram
Enlarge 200%**

Materials

Fabric: assorted cottons for motifs
    backing: 11½" square
    outside borders: 5½" x 2¼" (2); 2¼" x 8½" (2)
    center patch: 5½" square
Cotton batting: thin bonded, 9½" square
Needles
Straight pins
Thread: coordinating
Embroidery floss: coordinating
Beads: 6mm (8); 8mm (1)
Buttons: small (4); medium (2);
    large (2); decorative (2)
Iron and ironing board
Sewing machine
Tracing paper and marking tool

Button Butterfly

General Instructions

Basic Construction—pages 10–13
Embroidery Stitches—page 14

Assembly
¼" seam allowance

1. Cut out pieces 1–2.
2. Fold edges of pieces 1–2 under ¼". Press. Blind-stitch to center patch. See Placement Diagram.
3. Pin and sew side borders to center patch. Press.
4. Pin and sew top and bottom borders to center patch. Press.
5. Blanket-stitch around butterfly wings. See photograph.
6. Sew buttons and beads on butterfly. Straight-stitch antennas. Make a French knot at the end of each antenna.
7. Herringbone-stitch along top and bottom of borders. See photograph.
8. Layer backing, batting, and assembled quilt. Pin. Fold backing to front of quilt and straight-stitch layers together.
9. Hang as desired.

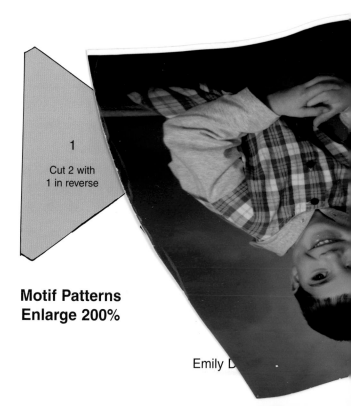

**Motif Patterns
Enlarge 200%**

1
Cut 2 with
1 in reverse

Emily D

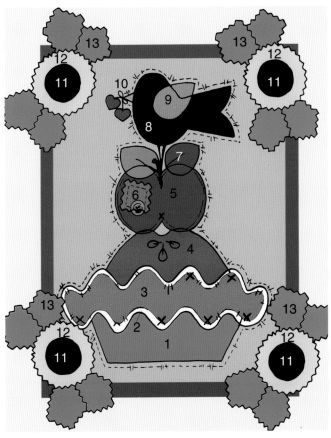

Placement Diagram
Enlarge 245%

Materials

Fabric: assorted cottons for motifs
    backing: 8¾" x 11¾"
    background: 8½" x 11½"
    center patch: 6½" x 8¾"
Cotton batting: thin bonded, 8¾" x 11¾";
    piece 12: 2" circles (4);
    piece 11: 1½" circles (4);
    piece 2
Fusible web
Iron and ironing board
Needles
Straight pins
Thread: coordinating
Embroidery floss: coordinating
Buttons: small heart (2); small round (1)
Permanent ink pen
Glue: fabric
Twigs: 11"; tiny twig for apple stem
Scissors
Pinking shears
Tracing paper and marking tool

Blackbird Pie

General Instructions

Basic Construction—pages 10–13
Embroidery Stitches—page 14

Assembly

1. Fray edges on backing, background, and center patch. Cut out piece 13 and fabric and batting for piece 11 using pinking shears. See additional pattern pieces on page 93.

2. Trace, apply fusible web to, and cut out pieces 1 and 3–10 according to General Instructions. Cut out batting for piece 2.

3. Cut out fabric and batting (4 each) for pieces 12 using pinking shears. Apply fusible web to all four fabric pieces of piece 12.

4. Fuse pieces 1 and 4–10 to center patch, following manufacturer's instructions. Fuse piece 3 to piece 2. Fuse all four fabric pieces of piece 12 to batting pieces of piece 12. See Placement Diagram.

5. Attach pie crust (pieces 2–3) to background with nine "X"-stitches.

6. Layer backing, batting, and background. Pin. Straight-stitch layers together. Straight-stitch assembled center patch to assembled quilt.

7. Layer piece 12, batting piece 11, and fabric piece 11. Attach to each corner by sewing an "X"-stitch in center of fabric piece 11. Sew pieces 13 under each side of flower.

8. Sew one small round button on apple. Straight-stitch veins on leaves. Sew on tiny twig for apple stem.

9. Make two lazy daisy-stitches for the bow under the blackbird's beak and straight-stitch for bow ends. Glue two heart buttons at the end of each straight stitch.

10. Outline stitches around motifs using a permanent ink pen.

11. Attach 11" twig for hanging.

   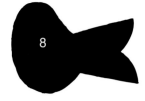

Motif Patterns
Enlarge 200%
Piece 10 • Full Size

Emily Dinsdale 87

Placement Diagram
Enlarge 200%

Materials

Fabric:
    backing: 6" x 8¼
    top patch: 5¾" x 1"
    bottom patch: 5¾" x 2¾"
    muslin patch: 5¾" x 4¾"
    piece 26: 7" x 2½"
    felt: 6" x 8¼";
        piece 28
Needles
Straight pins
Thread: coordinating
Embroidery floss: coordinating
Stencil brushes
Stencil paints: desired colors
Masking tape
Clear acetate or lightweight cardboard
Ribbon: ⅛"-wide, 6"
Buttons: small (3); medium (7)
Scissors
Pinking shears
Craft knife
Tracing paper and marking tool
Decorative mini hanger

Best Friends

General Instructions

Basic Construction—pages 10–13
Additional Techniques—page 13
Embroidery Stitches—page 14

Assembly

1. Cut out backing, felt, bottom, top and muslin patches, fabric for piece 26, and felt for piece 28 using pinking shears. See additional pattern pieces on page 94.

2. Stencil the two girls and flowers on muslin. Sew a small button on the neck of one girl. Sew a button on the waist and on the hair bow of the other girl. Tie ribbon in a small bow and stitch on stenciled flowers. Place three "X"-stitches on one girl's dress. Place two rows of straight stitches along bottom of other girl's dress. See Placement Diagram.

3. Layer backing, felt, and top patch. Attach by sewing four buttons across top patch. Place three "X"-stitches between buttons.

4. Layer piece 28 and 26 on bottom patch. Pin. Attach layers to backing and felt by sewing a button in the center of each heart. Place four "X"-stitches between and on each end of hearts.

5. Pin stenciled muslin, overlapping top and bottom patches. Straight-stitch along edges. Place an "X"-stitch in each corner of muslin patch.

6. Attach decorative mini hanger to the back for hanging.

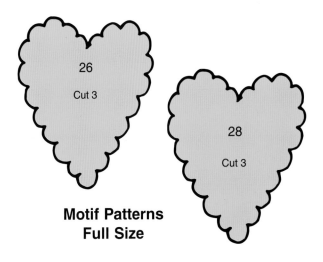

Motif Patterns
Full Size

Placement Diagram
Enlarge 200%

Primitive House

General Instructions

Basic Construction—pages 10–13
Embroidery Stitches—page 14

Assembly

1. Cut out pieces 1–8.

2. Pin piece 1 to background. Straight-stitch to background. Randomly stitch grassy areas. See Placement Diagram.

3. Pin pieces 2–6 to background. Blanket-stitch pieces 2–3 and 6 to background, and piece 4 to piece 2. Straight-stitch piece 5 to piece 2. Sew small button for door knob. Sew heart button on roof.

4. Glue piece 7 to background. Pin and straight-stitch around piece 8. Make French knots on tree for apples.

5. Straight-stitch smoke coming out of chimney.

6. Sew moon and star buttons to assembled quilt.

7. Place assembled quilt right side down. Place batting on top. Place back of frame on top of batting. Mount and secure in frame.

Materials

Fabric: assorted wool and felt for motifs
    background: flannel, 5" x 7"
Cotton batting: thin bonded, 5" x 7"
Needles
Straight pins
Thread: coordinating
Embroidery floss: coordinating
Buttons: stars (3); moon (1); heart (1); small (1)
Glue: fabric
Frame: wooden, 5" x 7"
Scissors
Tracing paper and marking tool

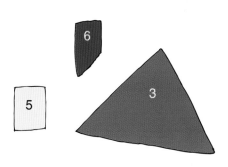

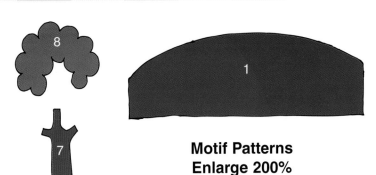

Motif Patterns
Enlarge 200%

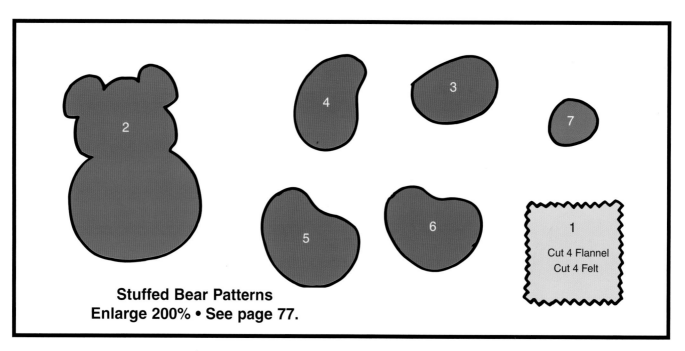

Stuffed Bear Patterns
Enlarge 200% • See page 77.

1
Cut 4 Flannel
Cut 4 Felt

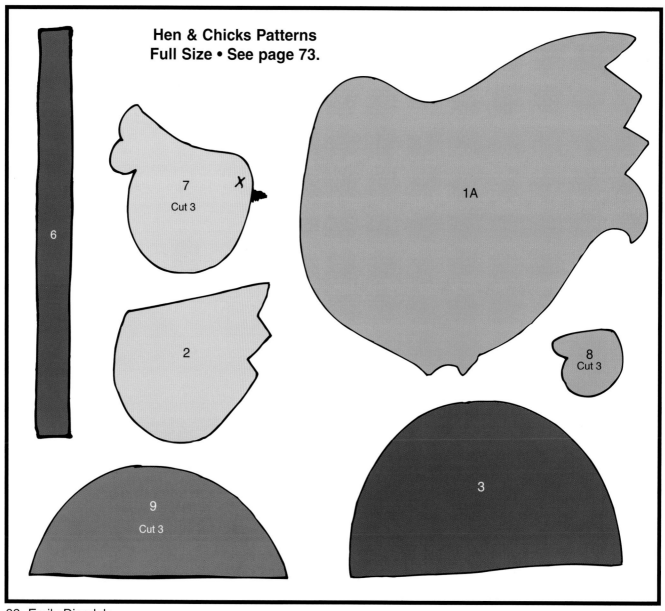

Hen & Chicks Patterns
Full Size • See page 73.

7
Cut 3

8
Cut 3

9
Cut 3

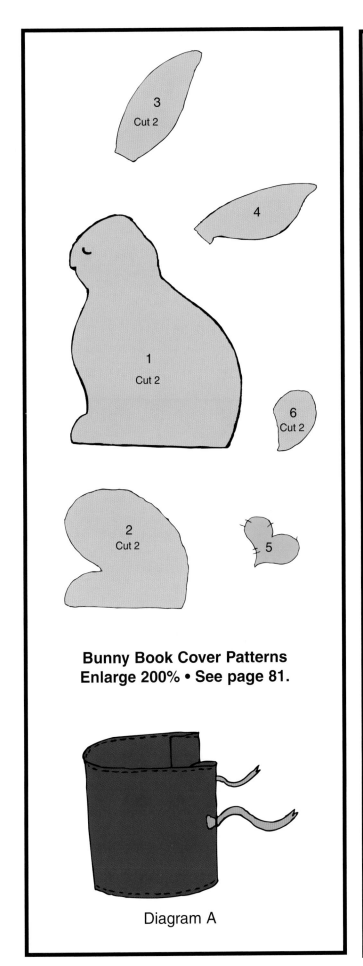

Bunny Book Cover Patterns
Enlarge 200% • See page 81.

Diagram A

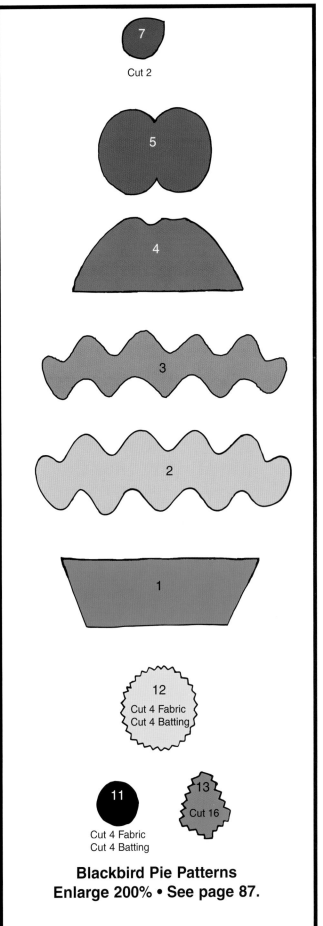

Blackbird Pie Patterns
Enlarge 200% • See page 87.

Best Friends Patterns
Full Size • See page 89.

1

2

24

15

25

4 5 6

3

14

16

7

8

13 17 27

9 10

11 12

18

20 21

19

22 23

**Apples
For Three
Pattern**

Autumn Time Pattern

Garden Fresh Pattern

Beehive & Strawberries Pattern

Honey Pot Pattern

Patches the Cat Pattern

Forest Friends Pattern

Signs of Spring Pattern

Victorian Charm Pattern

Rain Rain Go Away Pattern

Forget-Me-Not Pattern

Wish'n I Were Fish'n Pattern

Welcome Home Pattern

Angel In Flight Pattern

Girls Love Flowers Pattern

Sweetheart Sampler Pattern

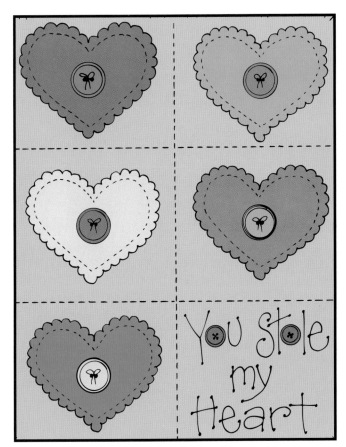

You Stole My Heart Pattern

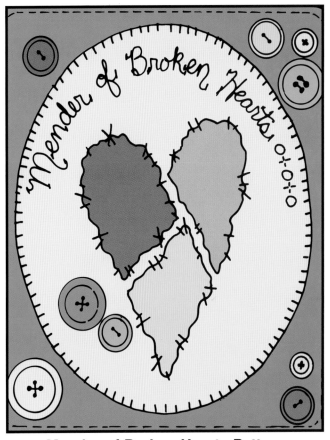

Mender of Broken Hearts Pattern

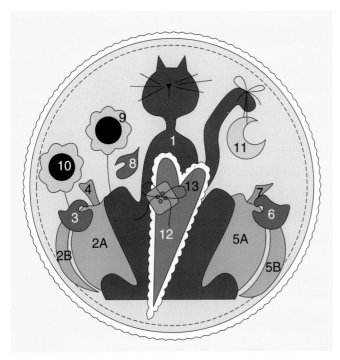

**Placement Diagram
Enlarge 250%**

Materials

Fabric: assorted cottons for motifs
   background: 8" circle
Cotton batting: thin bonded, 8½" circle
Fusible web
Iron and ironing board
Needles
Thread: coordinating
Embroidery floss: coordinating
Button: medium (1)
Sponge
Acrylic paint: desired color
Spray sealer: clear matte
Double-sided adhesive
Glue: fabric
Scissors
Pinking shears
Tracing paper and marking tool
Papier mâché box with lid: 9½"-diameter

Trick or Treat Box

General Instructions

Basic Construction—pages 10–13
Additional Techniques—page 13
Embroidery Stitches—page 14

Assembly

1. Sponge-paint top of lid. Let paint dry thoroughly. Spray with clear matte spray sealer.

2. Cut out 8½" circle and piece 13 from batting using pinking shears. See additional pattern pieces on page 116.

3. Trace and apply fusible web to background and pieces 1–12 according to General Instructions. Apply double-sided adhesive to pieces 14–19. Cut out pieces 1–12 and 14–19.

4. Fuse pieces 1–11 to background, following manufacturer's instructions. See Placement Diagram. Adhere pieces 14–19 to side of box, following manufacturer's instructions. See photograph.

5. Fuse piece 12 to piece 13. Attach assembled piece to cat by stitching on button.

6. Backstitch cat's nose and whiskers.

7. Stitch around cat's tail, loop around moon, come back up to top of cat's tail and tie a bow.

8. Sew a running-stitch around outside edge of quilt.

9. Fuse assembled background to 8½" circle of batting. Apply glue to batting and adhere it to center top of box.

10. *Note: This can also be used on a canvas bag for trick-or-treaters.*

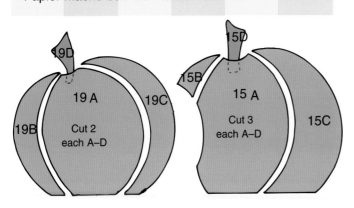

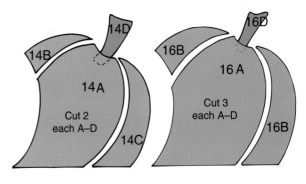

**Motif Patterns
Enlarge 200%**

**Placement Diagram
Enlarge 200%**

Materials

Fabric: assorted cottons for motifs
    background: 7" x 7"
    outside borders: 8¾" x 1¼" (2); 7" x 1¼" (2)
Cotton batting: thin bonded, 8" x 8"
Fusible web
Iron and ironing board
Needles
Straight pins
Thread: coordinating
Embroidery floss: coordinating
Scissors
Sewing machine
Tracing paper and marking tool
Pillow form

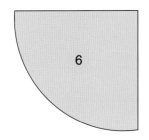

**Motif Patterns
Enlarge 200%**

Morning Rooster

General Instructions

Basic Construction—pages 10–13
Embroidery Stitches—page 14

Assembly
¼" seam allowance

1. Trace, apply fusible web to, and cut out pieces 1–6 according to General Instructions.

2. Fuse pieces 1–6 to background, following manufacturer's instructions. See Placement Diagram.

3. Sew side borders to background, right sides together. Press. Sew top and bottom borders to background. Top and bottom borders will overlap the side borders. Press. See photograph.

4. Pin batting to assembled background. Straight-stitch sun rays and rooster legs. Lazy daisy-stitch rooster feet, flower petals, and leaves. Straight-stitch flower stems. Make French knots for flower centers. Straight-stitch around rooster body. Remove pins.

5. Fold and press border edges under ¼". Sew assembled quilt to the top of a favorite pillow by blind-stitching around outside borders.

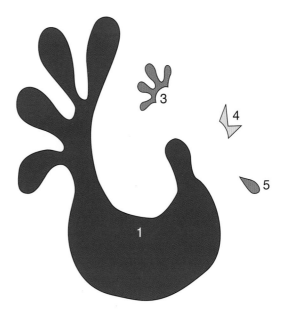

**Placement Diagram
Enlarge 175%**

Materials

Fabric: assorted cottons for motifs
    background: 6¾" x 8"
    pieces 1: 8" x 9"
    piece 2: 6" x 7"
    outside borders: 8" x 1¼" (2); 9½" x 1¼" (2)
Cotton batting: thin bonded, 6¾" x 8"
Fusible web
Iron and ironing board
Needles
Straight pins
Thread: neutral-colored
Embroidery floss: coordinating
Double-sided adhesive
Scissors
Sewing machine
Tracing paper and marking tool
Paper bag

Floral Bag

General Instructions

Basic Construction—pages 10–13
Embroidery Stitches—page 14

Assembly
¼" seam allowance

1. Trace and apply fusible web to pieces 1–2 and 6–7 according to General Instructions. Cut out pieces 1–8. See additional pattern pieces on page 117.

2. Fuse piece 1 to background, following manufacturer's instructions. Fuse piece 2 to piece 1. See Placement Diagram.

3. Sew side borders to background, right sides together. Press. Sew top and bottom borders to background. Press.

4. Layer batting and background. Pin. Fold outside borders under and blind-stitch layers together.

5. Sew a running-stitch around outside edges of piece 2 and around each outside corner of piece 1 using neutral-colored thread.

6. Gather bottom edges of pieces 3–5 and around piece 8. Pin pieces 3–5 and piece 8 in place. Turn raw edges under ⅛". Blind-stitch in place. Straight-stitch stamens from center of piece 8 to center of flower petals. Make a French knot at the end of each straight stitch. Straight-stitch stem.

7. Adhere assembled quilt to paper bag using double-sided adhesive.

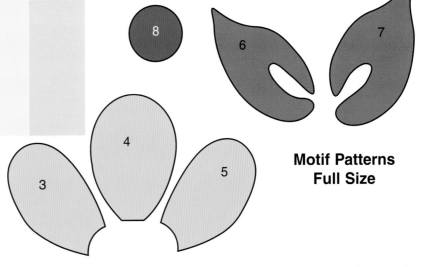

**Motif Patterns
Full Size**

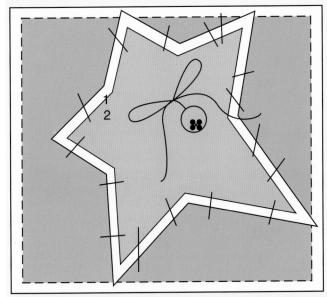

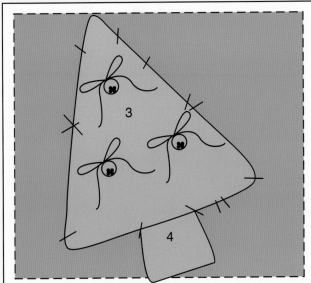

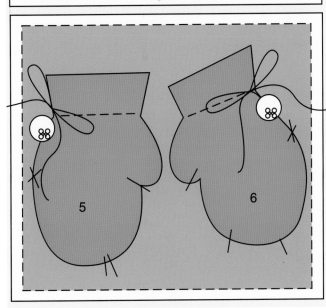

**Placement Diagrams
Enlarge 120%**

Ornaments

Materials

Fabric: assorted cottons for motifs
    backgrounds: 4" x 3½" (3)
    backings: muslin, 4" x 3½" (3)
Cotton batting: thin bonded, 4" x 3½" (3);
    scraps for motifs
Needles
Straight pins
Linen jute
Scissors
Tracing paper and marking tool
Decorative mini hangers: 4" (3)
Embellishments: as desired

General Instructions

Basic Construction—pages 10–13
Embroidery Stitches—page 14

Assembly

1. Fray edges on backgrounds.

2. Layer backings, batting, and backgrounds. Pin. Straight-stitch layers together using linen jute.

3. Cut out pieces 1–6 from motif fabrics and from batting. See additional pattern pieces on page 117.

4. Straight-stitch pieces 1–6, fabric and batting, to corresponding backgrounds. See Placement Diagrams.

5. Embellish as desired. Attach decorative mini hangers to the backs for hanging.

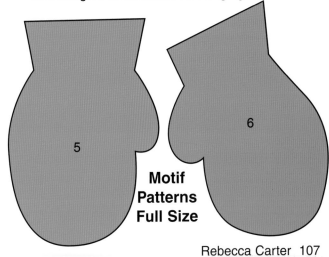

**Motif
Patterns
Full Size**

Rebecca Carter 107

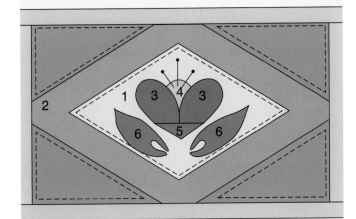

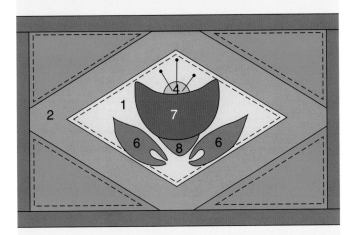

Placement Diagrams
Enlarge 200%

Materials

Fabric: assorted cottons for motifs
    backgrounds: 7" x 4½" (2)
    piece 1: 4" x 6" (2)
    piece 2: 5½" x 7½" (2)
    outside borders: 4½" x 1½" (4); 8¼" x 1¼" (4)
Cotton batting: thin bonded, 7½" x 5" (2)
Fusible web
Iron and ironing board
Needles
Straight pins
Thread: neutral-colored
Embroidery floss: coordinating
Double-sided adhesive
Scissors
Sewing machine
Tracing paper and marking tool
Corrugated cardboard cards: 5½" x 8" (2)

Quilt Cards

General Instructions

Basic Construction—pages 10–13
Embroidery Stitches—page 14

Assembly
¼" seam allowance

1. Trace and apply fusible web to pieces 1–2, 4, and 6 according to General Instructions. Cut out pieces 1–8. See additional pattern pieces on page 118.

2. Fuse pieces 2 to backgrounds, following manufacturer's instructions. Fuse pieces 1 to pieces 2. See Placement Diagram.

3. Sew side borders, right sides together, to background. Press. Sew top and bottom borders to background. Press.

4. Layer battings and backgrounds. Pin. Fold outside borders under and blind-stitch layers together.

5. Fuse pieces 4 and 6 to piece 1.

6. Gather bottom edges of flower petals (pieces 3 and 7) and around piece 5 and 8. Pin flower petals and pieces 5 and 8 in place. Turn raw edges under ⅛". Blind-stitch in place. Straight-stitch stamens from centers of piece 4. Make a French knot at the end of each straight stitch.

7. Sew a running-stitch around outside edges of pieces 1–2 and around each corner using neutral-colored thread.

8. Adhere assembled quilts to cards using double-sided adhesive.

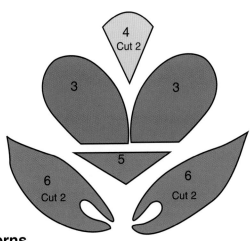

Motif Patterns
Full Size

Rebecca Carter 109

**Placement Diagram
Enlarge 200%**

Materials

Fabric: assorted cottons for motifs
    backing: 8¾" x 10¾"
    background: 7½" x 9½"
    straps: 4" x ½" (2)
Cotton batting: thin bonded, 7½" x 9½"
Fusible web
Iron and ironing board
Needles
Straight pins
Thread: coordinating
Embroidery floss: coordinating
Buttons: large (2)
Permanent ink pen
Scissors
Cinnamon stick: 9"
Tracing paper and marking tool

Moon Santa

General Instructions

Basic Construction—pages 10–13
Additional Techniques—page 13
Embroidery Stitches—page 14

Assembly

1. Fray edges of backing.

2. Trace, apply fusible web to, and cut out pieces 1–13 according to General Instructions. See additional patterns on page 118.

3. Fuse pieces 1–13 to background, following manufacturer's instructions. See Placement Diagram.

4. Place batting on back of assembled quilt. Pin. Backstitch tree trunk, pipe stem, smoke from pipe, and veins on holly leaves. Make French knots for stars and holly berries.

5. Outline inside of pipe using a permanent ink pen. Draw Santa's eye using a permanent ink pen. See Diagram A on page 118.

6. Layer backing behind assembled quilt. Pin. Fold backing to front of quilt. Straight-stitch layers together. See photograph.

7. Fold straps over and, using a button, attach to each corner for hanging. Hang with a cinnamon stick.

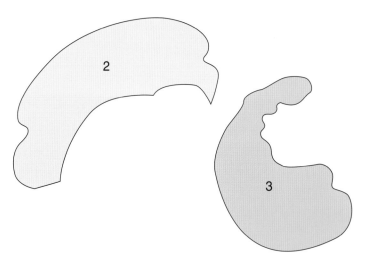

**Motif Patterns
Enlarge 200%**

Placement Diagram
Enlarge 200%

Materials

Fabric: assorted cottons for motifs
    background: 7¼" x 8¾"
    piece 16: 2" x 2½"
    piece 17: 4¼" x 2¼"
    piece 18: 3" x 4"
    piece 19: 3½" x 4½"
    patch behind lettering: 7" x 1½"
Cotton batting: thin bonded, 7½" x 9"
Fusible web
Iron and ironing board
Needles
Embroidery floss: coordinating
Button: small (1)
Permanent ink pen
Glue: fabric or double-sided adhesive
Pinking shears
Scissors
Tracing paper and marking tool
Sketch book: 8¼" x 11"

Sketch Book

General Instructions

Basic Construction—pages 10–13
Embroidery Stitches—page 14

Assembly

1. Fray edges of background.

2. Trace and apply fusible web to background and pieces 1–15 according to General Instructions. Cut out pieces 1–15. See additional pattern pieces on page 119.

3. Cut out batting, pieces 16–19, and patch for lettering using pinking shears. Apply fusible web to batting, pieces 16–19, and patch for lettering.

4. Fuse pieces 1–15 to patches, following manufacturer's instructions. Fuse pieces 16–19 (patches) to background. Fuse background to batting. See Placement Diagram.

5. Sew long, straight stitches for sun rays. Use a lazy daisy stitch for flower leaf. Make a French knot for center of flower. Backstitch flower stem and lettering. See Lettering Diagram on page 119.

6. Outline stitches around patches. Draw bees' stripes, bees' heads, and antennas using a permanent ink pen. Sew button on piece 11.

7. Adhere assembled quilt to front of sketch book using glue or double-sided adhesive.

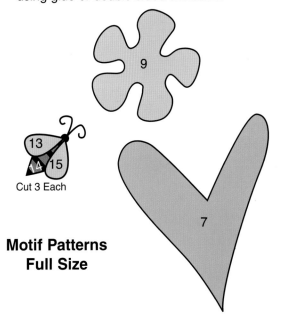

Motif Patterns
Full Size

**Placement Diagram
Enlarge 220%**

Materials

Fabric: assorted cottons for motifs
    patches: 4½ x 4½" (4)
    strips: 1¾" x 8"; 1¼" x 8"
Cotton batting: thin bonded, 8" x 10"
Fusible web
Iron and ironing board
Needles
Thread: coordinating
Straight pins
Embroidery floss: coordinating
Pencil
Scissors
Sewing machine
Tracing paper and marking tool
Frame: wooden, 8" x 10"
Foam mounting board
Masking tape

Cock-A-Doodle

General Instructions

Basic Construction—pages 10–13
Embroidery Stitches—page 14

Assembly
¼" seam allowance

1. Trace, apply fusible web to, and cut out pieces 1–4 according to General Instructions. *Note: Bottom right rooster is positioned in opposite direction.*

2. Sew patches, right sides together. Press open.

3. Sew two strips together along one long edge. Press open.

4. Sew strips along bottom edges of patches, right sides together. Press open.

5. Fuse pieces 1–4 to patches, following manufacturer's instructions. See Placement Diagram.

6. Layer batting and assembled quilt. Pin. Straight-stitch layers together. Make French knots on top left rooster. Straight-stitch roosters' feet.

7. Trace lettering with a pencil. Backstitch lettering. See Lettering Diagram. Sew rooster tracks along bottom strip using straight stitches.

8. Place assembled quilt right side down. Place mounting board on top of batting. Tape to secure. Mount and secure in frame.

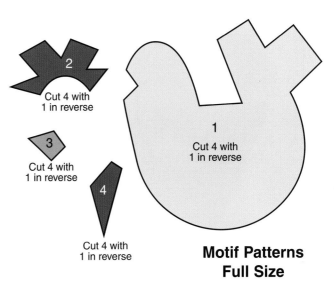

**Motif Patterns
Full Size**

COCK-A-DOODLE-DOO

**Lettering Diagram
Enlarge 200%**

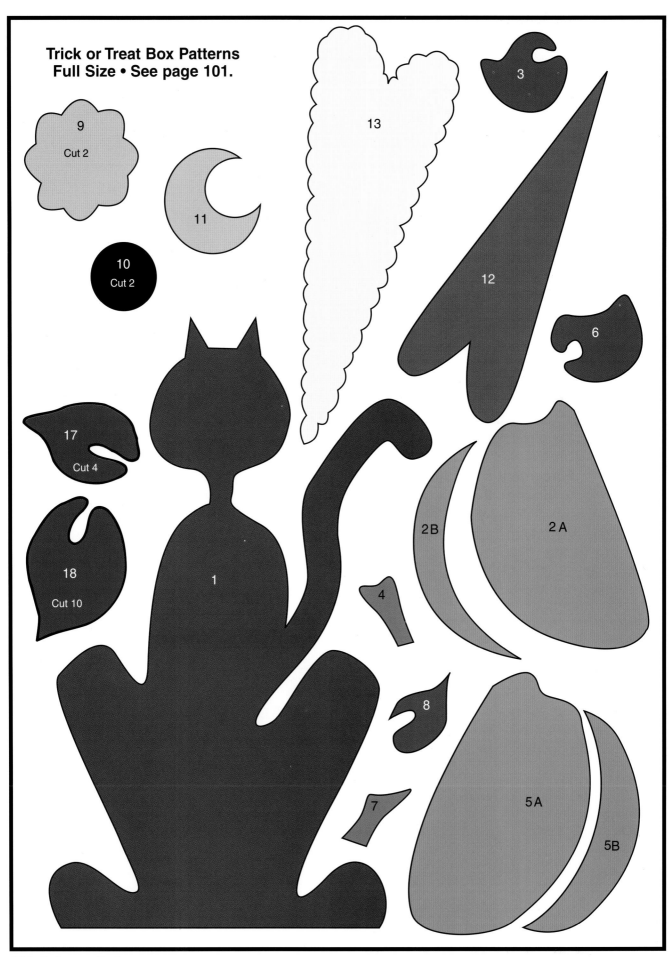

**Trick or Treat Box Patterns
Full Size • See page 101.**

9
Cut 2

11

10
Cut 2

13

3

12

6

17
Cut 4

18
Cut 10

1

2B

2A

4

8

5A

5B

7

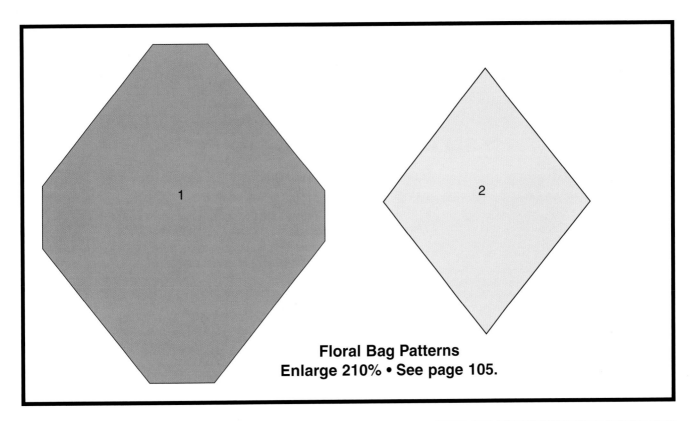

Floral Bag Patterns
Enlarge 210% • See page 105.

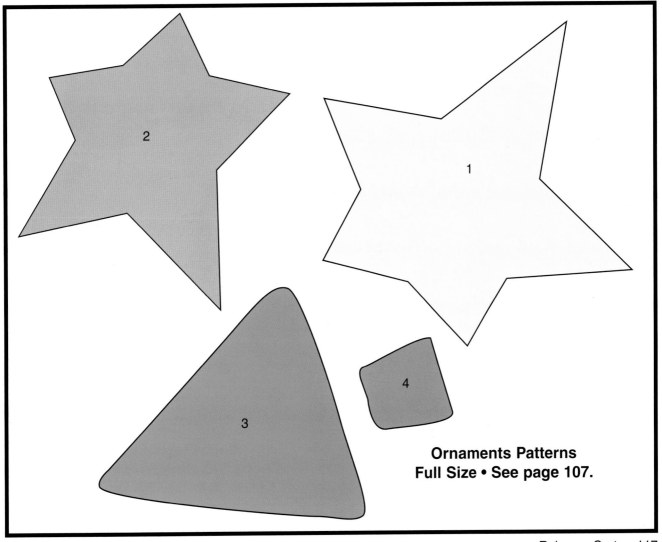

Ornaments Patterns
Full Size • See page 107.

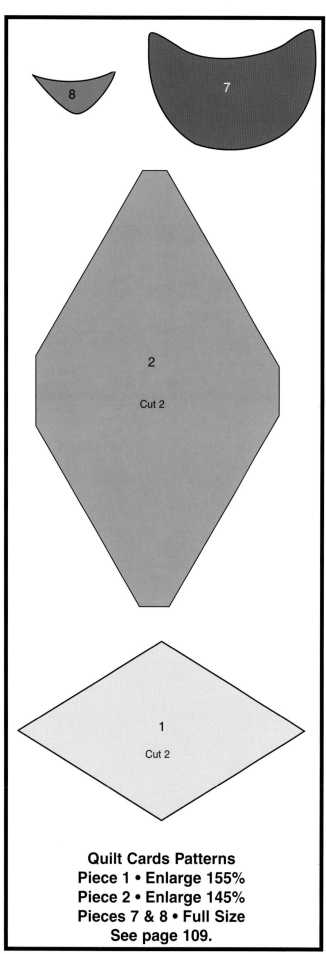

Quilt Cards Patterns
Piece 1 • Enlarge 155%
Piece 2 • Enlarge 145%
Pieces 7 & 8 • Full Size
See page 109.

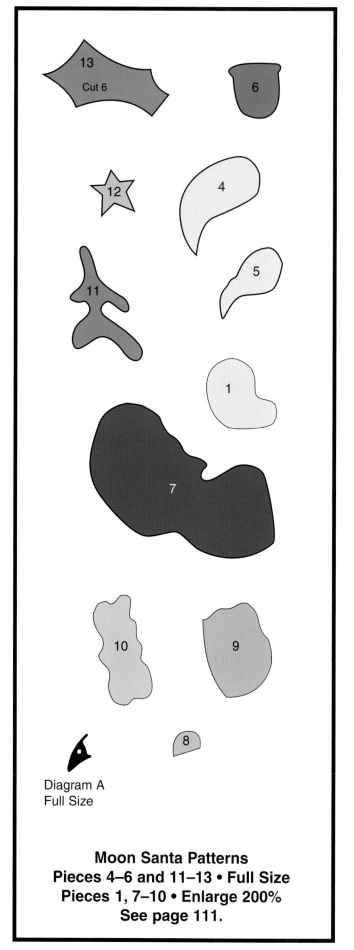

Diagram A
Full Size

Moon Santa Patterns
Pieces 4–6 and 11–13 • Full Size
Pieces 1, 7–10 • Enlarge 200%
See page 111.

Sketch Book Patterns
Full Size • See page 113.

Lettering Diagram
Full Size

Christmas Mittens Pattern

Crazy Patch Pattern

Patchwork Snowman Pattern

Tis' the Season Pattern

**Woodland
Night
Pattern**

Catch of the Day Pattern

Home In Heart Pattern

Home Is Where the Heart Is Pattern

Home Tweet Home Pattern

Raggedy Pals Pattern

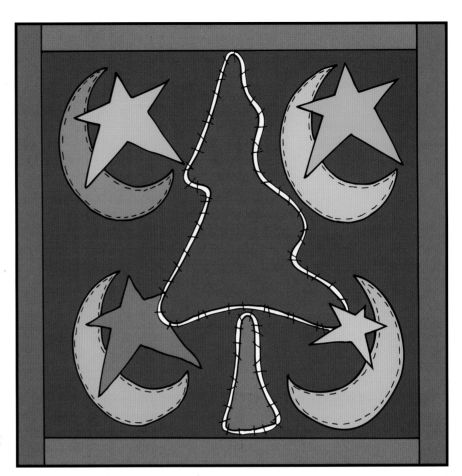

**Moon
Night
Pattern**

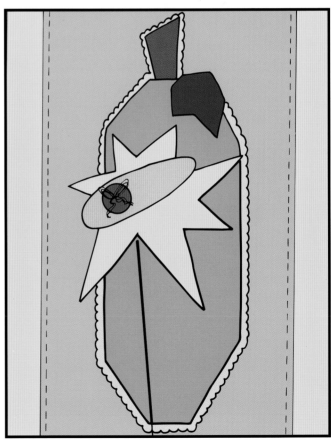

Scarecrow with Pumpkins Pattern

Pumpkin with Sunflower Pattern

Baby's Asleep Pattern

Warm Hands . . . Warm Heart Pattern

Barnyard Friends Pattern

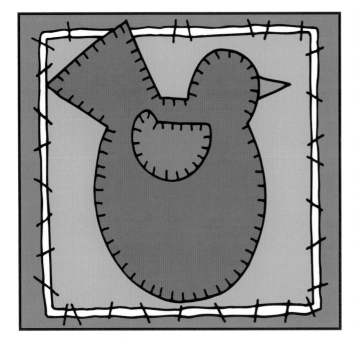

Country Bird Pattern

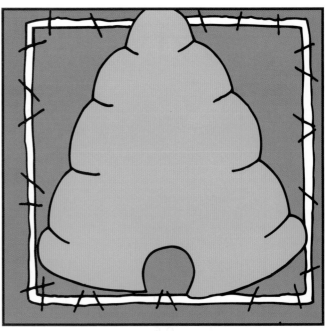

Country Beehive Pattern

Country Bee Pattern

Country Birdhouse Pattern

Metric Equivalency Chart

mm-millimetres cm-centimetres
inches to millimetres and centimetres

inches	mm	cm	inches	cm	inches	cm
⅛	3	0.3	9	22.9	30	76.2
¼	6	0.6	10	25.4	31	78.7
½	13	1.3	12	30.5	33	83.8
⅝	16	1.6	13	33.0	34	86.4
¾	19	1.9	14	35.6	35	88.9
⅞	22	2.2	15	38.1	36	91.4
1	25	2.5	16	40.6	37	94.0
1¼	32	3.2	17	43.2	38	96.5
1½	38	3.8	18	45.7	39	99.1
1¾	44	4.4	19	48.3	40	101.6
2	51	5.1	20	50.8	41	104.1
2½	64	6.4	21	53.3	42	106.7
3	76	7.6	22	55.9	43	109.2
3½	89	8.9	23	58.4	44	111.8
4	102	10.2	24	61.0	45	114.3
4½	114	11.4	25	63.5	46	116.8
5	127	12.7	26	66.0	47	119.4
6	152	15.2	27	68.6	48	121.9
7	178	17.8	28	71.1	49	124.5
8	203	20.3	29	73.7	50	127.0

yards to metres

yards	metres	yards	metres	yards	metres	yards	metres	yards	metres
⅛	0.11	2⅛	1.94	4⅛	3.77	6⅛	5.60	8⅛	7.43
¼	0.23	2¼	2.06	4¼	3.89	6¼	5.72	8¼	7.54
⅜	0.34	2⅜	2.17	4⅜	4.00	6⅜	5.83	8⅜	7.66
½	0.46	2½	2.29	4½	4.11	6½	5.94	8½	7.77
⅝	0.57	2⅝	2.40	4⅝	4.23	6⅝	6.06	8⅝	7.89
¾	0.69	2¾	2.51	4¾	4.34	6¾	6.17	8¾	8.00
⅞	0.80	2⅞	2.63	4⅞	4.46	6⅞	6.29	8⅞	8.12
1	0.91	3	2.74	5	4.57	7	6.40	9	8.23
1⅛	1.03	3⅛	2.86	5⅛	4.69	7⅛	6.52	9⅛	8.34
1¼	1.14	3¼	2.97	5¼	4.80	7¼	6.63	9¼	8.46
1⅜	1.26	3⅜	3.09	5⅜	4.91	7⅜	6.74	9⅜	8.57
1½	1.37	3½	3.20	5½	5.03	7½	6.86	9½	8.69
1⅝	1.49	3⅝	3.31	5⅝	5.14	7⅝	6.97	9⅝	8.80
1¾	1.60	3¾	3.43	5¾	5.26	7¾	7.09	9¾	8.92
1⅞	1.71	3⅞	3.54	5⅞	5.37	7⅞	7.20	9⅞	9.03
2	1.83	4	3.66	6	5.49	8	7.32	10	9.14

Index